Kyoshin

An Introduction to Jodo Shinshu

Volume 1: The Salvation of Jodo Shinshu and its Structure

Translated by John Iwohara

Kobozu (The Little Priest) Publishing

Originally Published in Japanese as *Shinran no Hihan Seishin*

© 1988 Kyoshin Asano

Kobozu (The Little Priest) Publishing

Copyright © 2013 John Iwohara

ISBN: 0984823220
ISBN-13:9780984823222

TABLE OF CONTENTS

Appendix

FORWARD

Recently, even while we are at peace, societal circumstances are such that we are in a period where we find ourselves caught up in the flow of globalization and are being pushed closer into unthinkable situations. However, even if we don't think in such a grand scale and look more locally these situations occur around us incessantly. In this situation, we are to experience the reality of causes and conditions, impermanence, and suffering that was delineated by Sakyamuni. Being within these circumstances as a human being is something that causes us to reflect deeply.

This short publication is a compilation of various essays and public presentations on the topic of death and intellect especially as it relates to the difficulties we experience as human beings. It is something that was written to try to find the attitude we should have in living in our current circumstances especially as seen within the teachings of Shinran Shonin. I was encouraged to publish by my colleagues as well as through the personal circumstance of wanting to remember my late father's third year memorial service. Although every effort was made to make the contents of this book as simple as possible, it is probably filled with inadequate analysis. I would appreciate any comments that you would provide to me regarding those points of inadequacies.

Written on this 13 June, 1988
Kyoshin Asano

Part 1

The Meaning of Death

1 A FIRST WORD

We live in a religiously pluralistic world. Many religions co-exist before us. Within these religions, or the many options that are now available to us, we hope to find a place where we belong, a true place of refuge. What I am hoping to do with this book is to understand the teachings of the founder of Jodo Shinshu, Shinran Shonin, by reviewing his accomplishments and exploring how the teachings of Jodo Shinshu can be of benefit to all of us today.

Although the teachings of Jodo Shinshu are often abbreviated as Shinshu, the term Shinshu was not originally used to describe a particular school of Buddhism. Instead, each of the Buddhist traditions used the word "shinshu" to express how their doctrinal lineage was a true transmission of Sakyamuni Buddha's Enlightenment experience.

Shinran Shonin also used the terms Jodo Shinshu and Shinshu here and there in his writing. However, instead of using the term to refer to a particular school of Buddhism, he used the terms to mean the true and real teaching for *birth in the Pure Land*. In other words, Shinshu and Jodo Shinshu both refer to the salvation of Amida Buddha.

Despite this, however, the terms Jodo Shinshu and Shinshu are currently used to refer to the school of Buddhism that describes the experience of Shinran Shonin in his personal experience of Amida Buddha's salvation. Within the attitude of the Founder's declaration that Jodo Shinshu was the path that allowed him to fully live out his life—the path that was chosen by the Shonin and the one that he regarded as the ultimate salvation called Shinshu—we can discover this ultimate place of refuge. At the same time, however, changing perspectives, we can also discover in the path that the Shonin chose the process of the activities the Founder took in order to reach this point of salvation. In talking about the salvation of Amida Buddha as expressed by the teachings of Shinshu it goes without saying that the focus becomes the contents of what the Founder was able to reach in finding his place of refuge. Here I want to look at the process that he went through in order to reach this point of salvation as a hint to finding how we might be able to relate to this teaching ourselves.

2 THE FOUNDER'S LIFE AND ACTIONS

Shinran Shonin lived approximately eight hundred years ago as the son of Hino, Arinori and was born in the outskirts of Kyoto in the village of Hino. In the spring of his ninth year, he *left the mundane world* to become a monk at the temple known as Shoren-in and until the age of twenty-nine was a practicing priest of the Tendai Buddhist tradition at the monastery established by Saicho on Mount Hiei. However, while doing the practices of Mount Hiei he came to the awareness that through these practices he could not reach his goal of *becoming a Buddha*. In order to continue to seek out the *path towards Buddha-hood* he confined himself to the temple known as Rokkakudo. From this experience he would later seek out Honen Shonin and through this meeting he was able to gain the ultimate path that lead him towards *achieving Buddha-hood*. This *path of achieving Buddha-hood*, he would conclude, was universal. It was a path that allowed all beings to *achieve Buddha-hood*. This is what he called Shinshu.

The above is a short history of the Founder's life. If we were to divide this history into periods it can be divided into three parts. The first period would cover the time between the Founder's birth and his leaving the secular world at the age of nine. The second period would be the time between his leaving the secular world until his departure from Mount Hiei at 29 years of age. The third period would be from the time of his seclusion at Rokkakudo until his achieving the path of Buddha-hood through Jodo Shinshu.

Furthermore, within this analysis of his life, at a very minimum it becomes clear that (1) like us, the Founder's birth was to a family found within general society; and (2) while being a part of general society, he chose the path of becoming a Tendai Buddhist priest. In other words, we discover that the basis for entering through the gate of the Buddhist path can be found within our daily lives.

Given this fact, perhaps it is necessary to reconsider what meaning our daily lives have. In other words, what exactly is our daily life?

In living our lives day to day, because it occurs as a matter of fact, we rarely find a need to discuss it. On the other hand, however, if we were asked to describe what daily life is we find ourselves stumbling for an answer. In any case, if we were to bluntly express what living our daily life is then we might say, "living." If we were to further ask what is "living," then there are probably some who would answer by saying that it is to live for a particular goal. Others might dolefully answer that it does not matter what the answer is because I am already born. In this way, although the answers are all different for each person, what we can say about each one of these answers is that "action" is or was required regardless of whether or not there is a purpose. Because of this, what we can say about our daily life is that it is comprised of our actions. Thus, if we were to express it differently, our daily life would be our actions or what we would call the accumulation of our actions.

What exactly is this action? It is something that is not limited to just humans but includes other animals as well. If you were to ask why actions are taken, although here too there are probably many ways to understand the phenomenon, we could say that the reason why humans and other animals take action is to maintain balance. For example, if an animal feels thirst then that animal gives rise to the desire of drinking water. Following this desire, the act of moving one's arms and legs and mouth to drink water occurs. Once the desire to drink is fulfilled to an adequate degree the activity or action of drinking is halted. In other words, actions are taken to maintain balance: the reason for taking action is the disruption of that balance, and once that balance is restored the action is stopped. Further, these actions are not just limited to external bodily actions but also includes the internal, emotional (spiritual) actions as well.

Although it may seem strange to have introduced animals as part of this discussion there is a reason for this. The reason is because I wanted to make clear the huge and unique difference that human actions have from animal ones. For example, in thinking about the action of eating, animals simply act instinctively and act just to survive. Humans, too, also eat for the same reason as animals do and eat simply to fill their stomachs. However, in the case of humans, we do not simply devour our food but, it should be noted, we have also established certain rules of behavior or etiquette. Even when it comes to the items that we eat it is often not presented raw but is often prepared in a certain way. This preparation of our food also involves such things as knowing the ingredients, and having the know how and techniques of preparation. Furthermore, these techniques are preserved and passed along to others. In the case of animals there is no comparable learning involved and the act occurs naturally. In other words, our human actions do not stop at this animal level. Our behavior also involves activities such as discovery and the learning of these discoveries by others. Moreover, these discoveries and learned activities become the foundation for culture. Because of this, we can say that what makes human activities unique is that it gives rise to culture. We can also say that this is one of the unique characteristics of human behavior.

When we observe the daily lives of human beings through their actions, daily life becomes the accumulation of cultural acts. Even the life of Shinran Shonin until the age of nine can be understood in these terms. Our daily life, our reality too, can also be seen in this way.

For this reason, Shinran Shonin *leaving the mundane world* to *take the priesthood* at the age of nine—religious actions are one aspect of cultural actions—is one action that Shinran Shonin took to protect the balance of his life at that time. Because of this, the act of *entering the priesthood* can be understood as one of many actions that was developed to address both the physical and the emotional states of a person. This was later learned by Shinran Shonin.

If we consider what cultural activity is, it can be categorized in various ways. For example, it can be divided according to the field in which it was discovered or in the area in which it functions. For the time being let us categorize these cultural activities into the following domains: those discoveries that are made rationally, following physical laws, and contribute to the social welfare of humanity through the actions occurring within the field of science; those activities that are meant to protect the order of society, and maintain the harmonious relationships between people that occur within the field of morality; and the appreciation or creation of works of beauty that occurs within the field of art.

If we were to further consider religious activity as a separate domain, how would it compare? In contrast to science and morality or the cultural fields whose actions are founded upon what we may consider "rational," religious activities, we can say, are those that occur beyond what we could consider rational.

What is meant by occurring beyond rationality does not mean that it negates or contradicts rationality; I am not saying that religious behaviors are irrational. Instead, what I mean to say is that religious activities are those activities that occur when rationality alone is not sufficient to provide an answer.

The advancement of science, founded as it is on rationality, has been able to contribute greatly to the social welfare of humanity. Science has even helped us to understand and make clearer areas of pursuit—such as psychology, ethics and the arts—that we may not ordinarily consider scientific. Moreover, even with human life itself science has allowed us to live longer because of the development of medical science and advancements made in areas such as pharmacology. We even hear of things like the combining of life forms together that might become possible in the near future. However, even if we are to continue to prolong human life little by little, this cannot be the answer to the issue of death. In other words, with regards to the issue of death, even while we try to find ways to postpone it as long as possible, even if we were able to provide an explanation that was objective and theoretically sound, this explanation would still not be able to provide relief from the problem of "my death." Moreover, while death is something that must occur, it is, at the same time, something that we cannot predict. "My death," in other words, is the worry and despair that comes when we consider what will happen when we become completely separated or torn away from our current reality. It is the worry and despair that comes when we are forced to take the trip to the world of the after-life. This is something that cannot be answered through rational answers alone. In fact, it is probably impossible to solve the collapse of this balance through rational means alone. Religion, when it comes to this kind of situation, can be regarded as one kind of cultural action that can preserve or re-establish this balance.

On the occasion of the Shonin receiving the *ordination as an initiate into the Buddhist Order*, it is said that he composed the following poem:

The vain cherry blossom that believes there will be a tomorrow, will not the gale blow in the night?

This poem, even if it was not written by the Shonin and was attributed to him posthumously, still points to the fact that the reason for giving rise to the religious act of *entering the Buddhist Order* was because of the unease associated with death. Moreover, that he *entered through the gate* of Tendai Buddhism in order to become an initiate means that people of a previous era had already discovered the kinds of activities that the Shonin, through learning these activities, was now trying to use in order to maintain his balance.

In this way, we come to understand that our daily life is the accumulation of different cultural actions of which religion is one of those domains of activity. Moreover, the religious world—a world that transcends the rational or a world that moves beyond the logic of the intellect—tries to solve, in particular, the unbalance caused when we directly confront death. We also come to know that even Shinran Shonin, who experienced the salvation of Jodo Shinshu, left the secular world in order to try to solve this problem of death. If this is the case, then the religious sphere of activity and in particular what has come to be called the salvation of Jodo Shinshu becomes something that has to be experienced personally as an individual. It is something that has to be heard by the individual and cannot be something done together with others. If you ask why, it is because death is something that occurs to each of us as individuals and is not something that we can experience together.

3 WHAT IS DEATH?

I am characterizing the chief characteristic of religion as the solution to the challenge of death. However, what exactly is this thing we call death? I ask this question, although it probably goes without saying, because even within our daily lives we are constantly confronted by "it." We experience the death of the physical body through such things as the death of someone in the neighborhood or by the death of animals and plants. Because of these experiences we say, "Yes, this is what is called death." Death, in other words, is something that we have come to know all too well. On the other hand, if we were to consider what this thing we feel we have experienced all too often is, then there are two separate cases to consider.

The first case we should consider is what we have generally come to consider as death. This is the death that is attended by a mortician; it is the physical death that each and every one of us must confront. This physical death is something that we must directly face but once; it is something that anything with life cannot escape. This physical death is the condition where the intellectual, emotional and spiritual activity of a human being is completely halted and never again to regain activity. It is, one can say, the catastrophic end of life. The second case to consider, although it has a somewhat forced meaning, is what we have come to call intellectual, emotional or spiritual death. Although explaining the contents of these different kinds of "death" becomes complicated, this is the death where parts of, or the totality of the functions we consider human are stopped even while the body is still able to function. This second type of death is somewhat different because it does not have the inevitability of the first kind of death. Because of this, the nature of this death is a little different. Despite this difference, however, what both types of death share in common is the fact that neither of these deaths is something that we can predict when it will occur for any given person. When we say that human life has been extended it does not mean that this is something that we all share in common. Instead, it is a calculated average. It does not mean, for example, that everyone will live to be eighty years of age. Furthermore, the coming of death does not distinguish between the old, the young, the good or the bad. It is something that attacks all unexpectedly.

4 THE MEANING OF DEATH—
NOTHINGNESS AND *EMPTINESS*

Although death can be seen as occurring in these two different ways, if I were to continue this discussion based on the first, more general understanding of death it is something that is not limited to humans but is something that all living things cannot escape. Again, this too, is also something that we cannot predict when it will occur.

When we take the perspective of the third person in considering what death is, we are unabashedly able to write explanations as found above. But, when it becomes "my death" can we really write in this way? Although it is true that death is the cessation of all physical and what we might call all "human" activity, if we were to wonder whether or not we can simply accept this statement as is, that death is simply the cessation of activity, we discover that we probably cannot. Even with regards to the fact that death comes unexpectedly and without a schedule we find it very difficult to simply accept this fact. Instead, all sorts of complicated musing and emotional upheavals are sure to arise. At this point, for humans, this disgusting thing called death, this harsh reality becomes something we have to figure out how to deal with within the framework of our daily lives. For many, the absolutely necessary world of religion, a world that cannot be ignored, opens up.

From here, we need to consider what meaning accepting this harsh reality of death holds. First, if we were to try to accept death from a very intellectual or outwardly logical point of view, it would be what was described up to this point. The meaning of death would be the stoppage of all the different activities that we identify with being a human being. Because of this, we could say that the human being has returned to a state of *nothingness* and is transformed into an *empty existence*. This perspective sees death as the conclusion of birth. Death is seen as being on the opposite side of life. The difference between life and death is seen as the difference between *existence* as opposed to *non-existence*. As *non-existence* death is seen as the contents of an empty box. Because of this, death is understood as something hollow. When we observe death as it occurs in our reality, it is true that we will find the cessation of all human activity. If the body is cremated, for example, all that is left is ash. Nothing else is left. Because of this, from a very human perspective, one way to understand death is as a very empty thing.

Although we probably do not think that this understanding of death is incorrect, at the same time we probably do not find any solace in this understanding either. If we were to accept this very straightforward understanding as the resolution to the problem of death, then as a reaction to this we could very easily fall into the trap of hedonism. We would say things like, "You can't see the flowers after you're dead" or "Life is short, you have to live it up." We would see our existence like the blooming flower and without any sense of responsibility we would abusively live for the moment or live our entire lives just seeking out what is pleasurable. In this way, the resolution that could have occurred with the imbalance caused by death is lost, and instead the whole of human life becomes a tragic loss.

5 THE MEANING OF DEATH— *IMPERMANENCE*

With regards to death, although it does mark the end of human life, we can also see it as the truth that pierces through our world and that appears as part of our humanity. This is the truth that Sakyamuni Buddha discovered; it is what has come to be known as *impermanence*. Thus, death is not the only thing that is *impermanent*. Human life itself is *impermanent*. In other words, *impermanence* does not first reveal itself with death. Getting old, getting sick, even achieving birth is *impermanence*. If the pain and suffering that comes from *impermanence* can be overcome through practice, then even while being impermanent one is no longer troubled by *impermanence*: the world of *true tranquility* opens up. Here, it is said that the issue of death is overcome. If one is able to achieve this perspective of overcoming *impermanence* then the entire world becomes a place of equality and the person who achieves this status is called an *awakened person* or a Buddha.

Providing a little more explanation on the issue of *impermanence*, however, things like our taking action in order to try to recover from our imbalance, and even growing day to day are all founded on the principle of *impermanence*. All these things, in fact, only become possible because of *impermanence*. If all this was not a part of *impermanence* and everything was in stasis, then growth, unbalance, birth, sickness, aging and death would not exist. In our daily conversations we say things like, "You always look so good. You haven't changed one bit since the last time I saw you" as a means to praise the other person. On the other hand, however, saying "You haven't changed one bit since the last time I saw you" is an expression of stasis and therefore deviates from the principle of *impermanence*. Because of this, it is something that does not belong in our world and instead of praising the other person we have slandered the other person. In reality this *"impermanence"* is a foundational principle and is something that people cannot avoid. Unfortunately, ignoring *impermanence* is a habit (in Buddhist terms this would be called *self-attachment* or those contrivances we maintain for ourselves) we picked up from birth. We are stuck into thinking from a singular perspective: we see *impermanence* as occurring only when something breaks or is destroyed. Because we abhor this kind of *impermanence* we find ourselves hoping that all of our objects, those things with form, will last forever. In other words, we find ourselves desiring for permanence or stasis. We do not want things to ever breakdown. In fact, because of this desire we go so far as to convince ourselves that things are not *impermanent*. Unfortunately, however, regardless of how resilient an object may be, even something as hard as steel or diamond, nothing can escape from *impermanence*.

Here, instead of becoming *attached* to the idea that this *impermanent* life of ours is not *impermanent*, if we accept it as it is—as an *impermanent* thing—then upon our full understanding of *impermanence* we would be able to seek the permanent world of the truth that lies above. The permanence that is gained through becoming attached to *impermanent* objects as permanent things is not the permanence of truth. Ironically, the permanence of truth is a world that only reveals itself when *impermanence* is recognized and accepted as *impermanence*. In order to overcome this challenge of *impermanence* a path becomes necessary. This path is the path that Sakyamuni Buddha made clear. Right now, we can say that the motive that moved Shinran Shonin to abandon the home at the age of nine can be found here where this meaning of death can be sensed or the desire to learn the path that Sakyamuni Buddha before him was able to demonstrate as one that could effectively overcome this meaning of death as *impermanence*.

6 THE MEANING OF DEATH—DEATH AS ADJACENT TO BIRTH

Earlier, when we considered the meaning of death from an intellectual perspective, we came to an understanding that birth is seen as a distinct entity and that death is that which comes from the "other side." We see the conclusion of birth as death and perceive birth and death as existing along a straight line. We also discussed how death is not something that we can predict or determine when it will come from "over there." Although we are not able to predict when death will come, we still try to create a certain distance between birth and death. Despite not being able to determine a distance between birth and death, we still find ourselves creating an arbitrary line that we have come to call the "average life expectancy." However, given that we cannot predict when death will come can we for certain say that this distance from birth to death is going to be something like thirty years, or ten years, or one year or even one month from now? If we were to carefully consider things, the very fact that we cannot predict when death will come means that we need to consider how wide this gap between birth and death really is. In other words, instead of being "over there" we can also consider how death might be right up against and adjacent to birth. Saying it more directly, we should not consider birth and death as separate entities. Having said that, however, birth and death are not the same thing. Therefore, what we are calling death, at this point, is not what appears on the other side of this arbitrary lifespan called human life but is something that exists side-by-side with the life that we have in the present moment. Moreover, this life can also be said to be possible because of death. If we were to become aware of this then we would discover that without the overcoming of death itself we would lose the meaning of life itself: we become aware that just considering life at the expense of death leads to a very one-dimensional understanding. Thus, the overcoming of death also has the meaning of overcoming life. Living completely is also dying completely; dying completely is also living completely. For this reason the overcoming of death is something that has to be done in the present moment. In other words, overcoming death is done while one is still living. Seeing death as being side-by-side with life also makes it easier to consider how death has the meaning of *impermanence*. We discover that death has the same meaning as *impermanence*.

This thing called death, from times past, has also been called the single most important thing in life. For Shinran Shonin what most vividly illustrates this point would be the poem introduced earlier or,

"The vain cherry blossom that believes there will be a tomorrow, will not the gale blow in the night?"

The resolution of death, as mentioned earlier, was something that Shinran Shonin attempted to accomplish through the tradition and practice of Tendai Buddhism. This path to resolution, although it was what he practiced for twenty years living on Mount Hiei, in the end was unable to resolve the issue of death for Shinran Shonin. As a result he left the mountain. Then, through the teaching of Honen Shonin, he looked towards the salvation of Amida Buddha and through this was able to discover at long last the salvation that he was seeking or the resolution to the issue of death, the same death that made life possible. This was different from an intellectual understanding and was neither the returning to *nothingness* nor becoming something that was *empty*. This was the discovery that birth into the world of Amida Buddha had the meaning of death. Likewise, discovering the meaning found within the resolution of death in life, while having the meaning of being a path to the world of Amida Buddha, was also a path that invested the seeker with a new destiny for humanity. It was a discovery that saw life as an adornment. This new way of looking at humanity also became the push towards the realization of peace in this world.

7 THE MEANING OF DEATH—
BIRTH-AND-DEATH (CONFUSION)

As written previously, although we attempted to understand the meaning of death—the death that we must without fail confront—if we were to do this from the perspective of Shinran Shonin's understanding we discover that there is one more way to understand death. This way of thinking is not to see death as the opposite of birth, but to combine it into the single compound word *birth-and-death* and use it as a means to describe confusion or suffering. Expressions such as *"transmigrating through the house of birth-and-death"* (Chapter on Practice), *"the ocean of birth-and-death"* (Chapter on Faith), *"birth-and-death is nirvana"* (Verses on the True Faith), *"the ocean of suffering of birth-and-death"* (Hymns on the Masters, Passages in Lament of Differences), *"the long night of birth-and-death"* (Meaning of the Textual Passages on Only Having Faith) are all examples of this.

The compound term *"birth-and-death"* that is being used here is not simply the unification of the opposite concepts of birth and death, but the repetition of birth and death. It is the falling and being carried by or the wandering about through *birth-and-death*. It is a term used in contrast to Enlightenment. Because of this, although there is no mistake that death is what follows birth, it is not something that is separate from birth. It includes both birth and *birth-and-death*. It is a term that tries to describe for us the state of confusion or suffering. *Birth-and-death* has this meaning.

This understanding is not unique to Shinran Shonin. It is something that is held by all the schools of Buddhism. The expression "*birth-and-death is nirvana*" is representative of this.

In particular, although it is also found within the traditional understanding of the Pure Land Schools, for Shinran Shonin this human lifetime is one of the *six paths¹*. The *six paths* are the paths that lead to the worlds of *hell*, the world of the *hungry ghost*, the *animal* world, the *warrior* world, the world of *human beings* and the world of *heavenly beings*. Taken together, these *six paths* describe the realm of confusion. Presently, the fact that we are in the world of human beings or one of the worlds of *birth-and-death* indicates that we have been wandering through the worlds of confusion from an indeterminate past. Because of this, if we were to just pass through this lifetime by simply performing worldly activities, then the future will continue forever as a wandering through the worlds of *birth-and-death* (confusion). Suffering, as a matter of course, will continue. Because we are burdened by this past, the fundamental meaning of birth as a human being becomes the ability to understand the present, even while being a part of a present that is filled with confusion, in such a way so that we will be able to bring in a future that allows us to gain a path that will allow us to transcend the worlds of confusion.

The death that was written about earlier, including the perspective of considering death as *impermanence*, is in reality the state of not grasping onto *impermanence* as *impermanence*. It is, in other words, trying to point exactly to the confused perspective of considering something *impermanent* as something permanent. We should deeply consider this.

Part 2

The Distinctive Features of Jodo Shinshu

1 THE STRUCTURE OF SALVATION

The activities that Shinran Shonin engaged in during his lifetime and in particular if we take his *abandoning the world* and becoming a monk, or the search through the domain of religion, as central to his experiences, then we will come to understand that the true task of religion is to overcome the unbalance that is created when we confront death. We have also come to know that overcoming the unbalance of death is also the resolution of death itself and that this becomes the resolution to the single most important matter of our lifetime. Moreover, especially with regards to the Shonin, death is not filled with malaise but is the going to be born into the world of Amida Buddha. Finally, we have also come to observe that it is within this context that his life in the present was adorned or decorated and that his true life as a human being was realized.

In this way, Shinran Shonin was able to realize the path that overcomes death in an efficacious manner. This, in other words, is the salvation of Amida Buddha. This salvation is Shinshu or more accurately Jodo Shinshu.

Having said all this, what exactly is this salvation of Amida Buddha? Because this is an important question to answer, I would like to answer this question by elucidating the distinctive features of the salvation of Amida Buddha as experienced and made clear by Shinran Shonin.

Although I am sure that there are various perspectives from which to elucidate this, I would like to begin by exploring it from two different perspectives. The first is the salvation of Amida Buddha or the salvation through the *Buddha's power*. This is also referred to as the salvation through *Other-power*. The second perspective is that of how the salvation of Amida Buddha is facilitated through the Buddha's world or the Pure Land. This aspect of salvation (*going to be born*) is described as the teaching of *going to be born in the Pure Land*, or again as *birth into the Pure Land*. Moreover, because Shinran Shonin saw *going to be born* as achieving the same Enlightenment as Amida Buddha this second point also becomes the salvation of *going to be born is becoming a Buddha*, or the salvation where we become a Buddha at the same time we are born into the Pure Land.

The Salvation of Other-Power

The teaching of Jodo Shinshu that was spread by Shinran Shonin is the teaching of being saved through the efforts or power of Amida Buddha. Given that this is an expression of the core belief there may not be a need to go beyond this statement. In reality, however, there is a very important meaning to be found here.

What I am saying is that through this salvation of Amida Buddha the Shonin was able to resolve the issue of death. This was something that he was not able to do in his twenty years of practice atop Mount Hiei. Of course, the Buddhist practice of Mount Hiei also has the objective of resolving death, but it is through the methodology that has been transmitted through the school of Buddhism known as Tendai. In other words, this approach is based on the practice of self-effort or *self-power*. In the case of the Shonin, even as he tried to successively perform these practices as prescribed by this methodology, the resultant state that he was seeking (the state of resolving death) did not appear before him. There were times when the resolution seemed to appear before him, but the resolution that he gained would quickly disappear and leave him. All that was left for him to see was the self that could not free himself from the confusion of his *passion*[2].

In other words, even as Shinran Shonin performed practices one after the other, he conversely became aware of the futility of overcoming the depths of his own confusion. Moreover, while existing as someone who, regardless of what he did, could not remove this *passion*, he was driven into the impossible situation of absolutely having to free himself from this *passion*. He was placed before an absolutely dire and impossible dilemma.

In order to escape from this dilemma he undertook a one-hundred day meditative retreat at the Rokkakudo, a temple built under the auspices of the Prince Regent Shotoku who was able to live a truly Buddhist life while living a secular one. As Shinran Shonin devoted himself to reflection over these one-hundred days, on the sunrise of the 95th day he became aware of the path that would allow him to transform and exhaust his *passion* through the salvation of Amida Buddha. Already, at that time, at a location known as Yoshimizu in Kyoto, Honen Shonin was explaining the salvation of Amida Buddha. Upon seeking him out, Shinran Shonin was awakened to the possibility of having his *passion* transformed, not through his efforts but through the salvation of Amida Buddha.

One point that should be made here is that beginning with the Buddha of the East or Ashuku Buddha (Skt. Akṣobhya Buddha) the Buddha of the ten-directions, whose numbers are as great as the grains of sand of the Ganges River, each have their own land (Pure Land). Despite each of these Buddha also having the desire to have beings born in their land, Shinran Shonin resolved to seek out only the salvation of Amida Buddha. This resolve to seek out Amida Buddha's salvation is faith. That is, in order to have faith in just Amida Buddha could only mean that Shinran Shonin awakened to the fact that the *passion* that we have as human beings could only be completely transformed by this particular Buddha's salvation.

Thus, the path of transforming our *passion* that the Shonin was able to realize is not based on our practice. Instead, because it is founded completely on the *Buddha's efforts* it is called the "salvation of *Other-power*." Because of this, what is referred to as *Other-power* is the effort by the Buddha to save *sentient beings*. Anything other than this cannot be called "salvation of *Other-power*." Furthermore, in Shinshu, this expression "salvation of *Other-power*" is used only to refer to the salvation of Amida Buddha.

Stated more carefully, "salvation of *Other-power*" is the "*salvation by the transference of merit of Other-power*." Generally, "*transference of merit*" refers to the exchange and application of merits earned through good acts towards the goal of becoming a Buddha. Originally, the term had this meaning of expecting to reach the goal (Buddha-hood) through this process of exchanging and applying the merits earned. However, what is called *"transference of merit of Other-power"* by Shinshu is Amida Buddha transferring the merits accumulated by the Buddha to we *sentient beings* for the purpose of allowing us to *go to be born into the Pure Land*. Amida Buddha allows those of us who cannot sever the ties to our *passion* through our own practice to *go and be born* into the Pure Land and has accumulated merits that will allow all of us to achieve the same Buddha-hood as did Amida Buddha. Because of this, as a matter of course, within those virtues are embedded the power to allow us to *go to be born* into the Pure Land which is unlike what is found within the general meaning of *transference of merit* that has an indeterminate nuance of "expecting" to achieve. In other words, this *transference of merit of Other-power* is a term used to describe the logic behind the inevitability of Amida Buddha's salvation. Within the *worlds of the ten-directions*, although there are innumerable Buddha, there is no other Buddha that employs this logic of the inevitability of the salvation of human beings.

The source of this inevitable salvation of human beings as expressed through *going to be born* is the Primal Vow of Amida Buddha. This Primal Vow is described within the Forty-eight Vows that can be found and is described in the foundational Sutra of Shinshu or the "Larger Sutra of Immeasurable Life." Within these Forty-eight Vows, the Eighteenth Vow is central. Therefore, expressing the salvation of Amida Buddha through the distinctive characteristic of the Primal Vow is done through using expressions such as *"salvation through the Other-power of the Primal Vow,"* and *"salvation through the Primal Vow of Other-Power."* Next, I would like to quote the Eighteenth Vow:

"If, when I become a Buddha, all the various people with a *true heart* have faith and rejoice, from the feeling of relief gained from going to be born with just the saying of the Nenbutsu and with this if these people are not able to be born in my country then I determine not to obtain Enlightenment. However, excepted are those that commit the crimes of the five transgressions or slander the True Dharma." (from interpretive version of the Three Pure Land Sutra)

Here, "all the various people...are not able to be born in my country" (birth of human beings) and "then I determine not to obtain Enlightenment" (the Buddha's True Awakening) are found together. This is to signify that the Buddha's Enlightenment is not complete without the birth of humans into the Buddha's Land. No other Buddha are found who have fulfilled this kind of Vow. Because Amida Buddha is this kind of Buddha, the Shonin determined that the path for salvation can only be found within the salvation of Amida Buddha or, in other words, can only be found within the salvation of the *Primal Vow of Other-power*.

Therefore, the *salvation by the transference of merit of Other-power* and the *salvation through the Other-power of the Primal Vow* are both expressions that describe the uniqueness of the salvation of Amida Buddha. The expression *salvation of Other-power* was originally used to specifically refer to the salvation of Amida Buddha. In the mundane world, however, this original meaning is ignored and some people carelessly and sporadically use the term "Other-power of the Primal Vow (Tariki Hongan)" while justifying their misuse as just being similar in form. This, however, is something that should be solemnly avoided.

The Salvation of Going to be Born is Becoming a Buddha

What exactly does it mean to be saved by the *Other-power of the Primal Vow*? How is this reflected concretely in our lives? The answer to these questions is at the same time you go to be born into Amida Buddha's world of the Pure Land you becomes the same Buddha as Amida Buddha. In other words, the answer to these questions is, "We become a Buddha." The world of Amida Buddha is the world where Amida Buddha exists. It is the Pure World that was established to save us *sentient beings* who cannot sever our own *passion*.

Generally speaking, the meaning that going to a Buddha's Pure Land has is to become a Buddha (achieving Enlightenment in *that* land). This is contrasted to becoming a Buddha in our temporal, material world (entering the sacred in *this* land). The former is called the *gate of the Pure Land*. The later is called the *gate of the path of sages*.

Originally, however, this idea of *going to be born into the Pure Land* was also something employed by those who took the perspective of the *gate of the path of sages*. This was because even if you were someone taking the *gate of the path of sages* and who excelled in wisdom, many recognized that with only the practices performed in this world it was still difficult to achieve Enlightenment. In order to fulfill the potential of Buddha-hood, these individuals desired to achieve Buddha-hood through continuing their practices even after being born in a Pure Land. In contrast to this, the *gate of the Pure Land* has as its goal *going to be born into the Pure Land* directly, and after achieving *birth in the Pure Land* to do practice to become a Buddha. This aspect of doing practice in the Pure Land is not unlike the *gate of the path of sages*. Regarding this *style* of the *gate of the Pure Land*, because you are able to achieve *birth in the Pure Land* through the *Buddha's Power*, it is like riding a ship over a water route to reach your desired destination. This is called the *path of easy practice* (the path that is easy to practice). In contrast to this, the *gate of the path of sages* is likened to walking over a land route in order to reach your destination because you try to become a Buddha by doing practices through your own effort. This is known as the *path of difficult practice* (the path of doing difficult practice). However, both paths desired *going to be born into the Pure Land*. The reason for this is because unlike doing practice in this temporal and material world that is filled with hindrances, the Pure Land is the *non-regressive* world where *retrogression* does not arise; it is a place where your efforts are realized without fail.

Although the above description is the general understanding of Pure Lands, and although the same term Pure Land is used, the world of Amida Buddha has a big difference in its personality. Of course, it goes without saying that it is a world without *retrogression*, but this world is one where together with *going to be born* it is also a world where you become a Buddha equal to that of Amida Buddha. It is a world where *going to be born is becoming a Buddha*. Thus, although it is a part of the same stream of the Pure Land tradition, the Pure Land of Amida Buddha is unique. It can be said that salvation through Amida Buddha's Pure Land is preeminent.

In this way, although the Pure Land teaching—and in particular the salvation of Jodo Shinshu—is one where you are able to achieve the ultimate status of Buddha-hood, this is all said to occur after our actual life has come to an end. With regards to this point, there are many who are critical. Their argument often makes the point that it does not matter what happens after death. What is important is the here-and-now. Or, as they sometimes also argue, talking about *going to be born* in the coming life is having expectations for an after-life. This expectation, they say, is nothing more than running away from the realities of life in the here-and-now.

However, although it is true that the salvation that Jodo Shinshu speaks of is done in terms of *going to be born* in the coming life, that is not to say that the here-and-now is abandoned. Similarly, *going to be born* in the coming life is not an explanation that is given to allow you to run away from the reality of the here-and-now. These criticisms, although at first glance may appear to be reasonable, do not have any relevance to the salvation of Jodo Shinshu. The reason for this becomes clear when we consider what this *here-and-now* that is placed in such high esteem really is.

In other words, this here-and-now is not something that comes into existence because of the here-and-now. Regardless of whether you are conscious of it or not, we are all headed towards the future. Conversely, the here-and-now is constantly being completed by the future. Because of this, trying to understand the here-and-now that does not take into consideration the future is a one-dimensional understanding. In terms of an analogy, it would be like a horse drawn carriage without a driver. As a passenger you would not know where you were going and because of this you could not help but to worry about what is going to happen. Or, even if you were to anticipate an assumed destination or future, it would only be an anticipation. It is only an anticipation because it is not something that will necessarily become the here-and-now. With these worries we become unsettled.

Those who simply look to see the here-and-now are those who have to live their lives in the middle of this kind of worry or unsettled existence. In contrast to this, those who are able to hold the coming world that is guaranteed by Amida Buddha in their hearts do not need to worry about this anxiety, or the unsettled feelings that come from not being able to see the future. Therefore, it becomes clear that the criticism against Jodo Shinshu that comes from this over estimation of the here-and-now is solved spontaneously. Again, using the same type of consideration as above, how can the path that Shinran Shonin took, one where human life is adorned, be considered ignoring the here-and-now and running away into the future? Although the logic may seem to jump, by holding a future image that transcends human life we are conversely able to appreciate the world that establishes the meaning of human life.

2 CLARIFICATION OF SALVATION (WHAT DO I HAVE TO DO TO BE SAVED?)

The activities of Shinran Shonin during his lifetime—his leaving the home, leaving Mount Hiei, and meeting with Honen Shonin—or his searching through the domain of religion and following the path he experienced as the salvation of Amida Buddha can also be described as the activities that enabled him to observe the flowering of human life through the salvation of Amida Buddha. The distinctive feature of this salvation, the flowering of human life, was expressed through the two points of "salvation of *Other-power*" and the "salvation of *going to be born is becoming a Buddha*." These unique features of "salvation of *Other-power*" and the "salvation of *going to born is becoming a Buddha*," because these are expressions that describe the salvation of Amida Buddha, can also be used to express and describe the entirety of Jodo Shinshu. However, within each of these expressions is found a particular focus. In other words, "salvation of *Other-power*" describes the source of the activity of salvation (what is being called Shinshu or the true essence) and *"going to born is becoming a Buddha "* is the description of how this activity of salvation is fulfilled or realized. This later phrase or *"going to be born is becoming a Buddha"* can also be thought of as an expression describing the final goal of the activity of salvation. Here I would like to make clear the full process of the salvation taught by Jodo Shinshu from the source of this salvation to its fulfillment.

With regards to making this process clear, although we can probably think of many ways to do this, I would like to do this by considering two separate interpretations expressed by Shinran Shonin. The first is indicated in the closing words of the Shonin's work titled "Meaning of the Text on the Single and Many Thought Moments." The passage is:

"The way of Jodo Shinshu is the *going to be born through the Nenbutsu*."

In this expression we find the path of salvation described in terms of the Nenbutsu. The other interpretation can be found in the beginning of the Shonin's chief work, the Kyogyoshinsho[3], in the Chapter on Teaching. The passage from the Kyogyoshinsho states:

"Deeply considering what Jodo Shinshu is, there are two types of *merit transference*. The first is the *form of going*, the second is the *form of returning*. With regards to the *merit transference of the form of going*, there is the true and real teaching, practice, faith and Enlightenment."

This passage talks to us about how we are saved through the *Faith* that is given to us by Amida Buddha as part of the Buddha's activity of *merit transference*. I would like to consider each of these points of interpretation separately, and then together.

Going to be Born Through Saying Namo Amida Butsu— Going to be Born Through the Nenbutsu

First, from the meaning found in the "Meaning of the Text on the Single and Many Thought Moments," Jodo Shinshu is what was *learned* from Honen Shonin or the *teaching* of *going to be born through the Nenbutsu*. This is the activity of saying Namo Amida Butsu aloud, and through this voiced utterance one goes to be born into the Pure Land. In this way, as a student of Honen Shonin, Shinran Shonin expresses how saying the Buddha Name of Amida Buddha (Namo Amida Butsu) is the path of being able to achieve birth in the Pure Land. It is this path, in particular, that allowed him to entrust the entirety of his being to and find peace in his life. Shinran Shonin declares that for him there is no other way.

The ease and universality of *going to be born through Nenbutsu*

Generally, the Nenbutsu can be largely divided into two distinct types. The first takes the form of the voiced utterance of Amida Buddha's Name. This Nenbutsu is one where your heart is devoted to the physical form of the Buddha or to the state of Buddha-hood. This is in contrast to the second form where through the *Nenbutsu of contemplation* or visualization you try to have the same heart as that of the Buddha. Of these two, performing the *Nenbutsu of contemplation* is extremely difficult. The Nenbutsu that is voiced is very easy. In other words, in order to perfect the *Nenbutsu of contemplation* you will have to go through a progression of various practices and because of this an extended period of time to accomplish these practices becomes necessary. More than just taking a long time to fulfill, you must also clear certain conditions found in the practice, without fail, to receive the benefits of that practice. Therefore, the *Nenbutsu of contemplation* as a path only becomes possible when a person who can clear these unique conditions appears. Because of this, it is practically impossible for the person who is weak of heart, foolish, without free time or without means to accomplish. In contrast to this, the Nenbutsu that is voiced is something that anyone can do. There is no distinction based on age or wealth. It is also the form of Nenbutsu that can be done easily anywhere. Furthermore, there is no need to even distinguish on the basis of mental abilities. It is something that anyone can do. Moreover, because it does not question the length of time necessary to accomplish, there is probably nothing easier to do. Finally, because this Nenbutsu that is voiced is easily accomplished, and because it can be done by all people it is clearly universal in its application.

This voiced Nenbutsu that is the *easy practice* (easy to perform) and is, at the same time, universal was within the historical transmission of Buddhism first pointed out by Nagarjuna[4] a man born in Southern India. Nagarjuna lived from about the middle of the second century C.E. His understanding of the Nenbutsu has been transmitted and then received by the three countries of India, China and Japan. This becomes one of the streams of Buddhism that continues to be taught today and holds as its principle the *going to be born into the Pure Land*. In particular, with regards to Shinran Shonin, this transmission that includes the three countries of India, China and Japan is part of the tradition of the Nenbutsu of voiced Nenbutsu. This lineage of transmission is made clear in Shinran Shonin's selection of seven great priests to include the aforementioned Nagarjuna Bodhisattva, as well as Vasubandhu[5] Bodhisattva of India; The Great Teacher Tan Luan, The Meditation Master Tao Cho, and The Great Teacher Shan Tao of China[6]; and The Regal Priest Genshin or Eshin and Honen Shonin[7] of Japan. Furthermore, we can say that this transmission also indicates the universality of *going to be born through Nenbutsu* that was received in a way that transcended time, country, and ethnicity.

The supremacy of *going to be born through Nenbutsu*

In the previous section I talked about how the *voiced utterance of the Nenbutsu* is both easy and universal. On the other hand, however, although the *voiced utterance of Nenbutsu* may have universal properties, if it can be done easily by anyone, then the question of its value comes into question. In other words, what we tend to ordinarily consider as valuable are those things that are difficult to come by. Things of value, we come to expect, are accompanied by many difficulties that have to be overcome before we are able to gain possession. Overcoming these difficulties requires much exhaustive effort before we are finally able to achieve our goal. If this is how we define something to be of value, then the *Nenbutsu of contemplation*, which is not easily done, would have to be considered valuable and superior. The *voiced utterance of Nenbutsu*, by contrast, is something easily done by anyone. By the above definition, this Nenbutsu would have to be considered as something without value and as being inferior. In order to make something inferior and of relatively little value into something that can be considered superior and with value you would have to bring together many of these inferior and relatively valueless items together, or so the thinking would go. Then, with this mindset, you start to become attached to quantity and begin to think of things like having to make fifty-thousand or sixty-thousand utterances of the Nenbutsu in the course of a single day. If we were to speak of this over an entire lifetime, then we would have to perform the *voiced utterance of the Nenbutsu* vigorously. If this becomes the case, then the distinctive feature of the *voiced utterance of Nenbutsu* as the easy practice is lost.

31

This kind of numerously repeated Nenbutsu is something based on the value system we find common in our world-view. However, if we were to explore the fundamental nature of the *voiced utterance of the Nenbutsu* that does not require vigorous repetition, then it is not simply just an easily performed act. Its value or position relative to other practices is also considered superior. In speaking about its superiority, however, we are told how we need to become aware that even as something superior there is nothing that can surpass it. The reason for this is because the *voiced utterance of the Nenbutsu* or saying the Name (the *Name-and-Title*) of Namo Amida Butsu is not simply the repetition of a name that has been affixed to a particular Buddha. Instead, it is a Name that has within it all the virtues that are necessary to bring us to the True and Real World of the Buddha. This is what we are given access to despite being someone who is constantly mired in confusion and cannot awaken to the True and Real. If we were to borrow the words of Honen Shonin, then "The *Name-and-Title* is the place of refuge of the tens of thousands of virtues." If we were to express what is meant by this we can use the construction of a house as an analogy. That is to say, in the example of fulfilling the practices necessary for the *Nenbutsu of contemplation*, or having to fulfill and build upon various kinds of practice and then coordinating the results of all those activities together until it leads to the fruition of the final desired result of Buddha-hood, then these individual practices necessary for the *Nenbutsu of contemplation* would correspond to the construction elements of a house. In other words, the individual elements such as the ridgepole, beams, cross beams and walls would all correspond to a particular practice necessary for contemplation. When all of these parts are assembled together and the the house is finally built, this is when, for the first time, you can say that the house of the *Nenbutsu of contemplation* is fully completed (or the *becoming a Buddha with this body* has been achieved).

In contrast, the *voiced utterance of the Nenbutsu* allows us to reach the goal of Buddha-hood, the same goal as that of the *Nenbutsu of contemplation*, with just the *voiced utterance of the Nenbutsu*. For this reason, the *voiced utterance of Nenbutsu* has to have all the elements that make up a house already within it. However, we should be careful to discern that it is not the activity of our saying the Name with our mouths that has the virtues that correspond to the house that we have been talking about. Instead, it is the Name itself, or that which we are repeating with our mouths, that corresponds to the house found in the analogy. It is the Name itself that has the value of all the virtues combined as *the house*.

In other words, the Name Namo Amida Butsu has within it not just all the virtues to have *sentient beings* reach the world of Enlightenment, which goes without saying, but has within it all the virtues of Amida Buddha placed within it. Accordingly, all the virtues of Amida Buddha as the Buddha of Salvation are placed within this *Name-and-Title* (all the virtues are given in the Name). I would go so far as to say that the manifestation of all the virtues of the Buddha is the *Name-and-Title*. Thus, the *Name-and-Title* is not just a title used to label a particular thing; it is distinct from being a code word used to distinguish between things. Instead, it is that which arose from the virtues of the Buddha of Salvation or Amida Buddha. The *Name-and-Title*, just as it is, performs the activity of salvation.

In contrast, in our world we put names on things and use them as labels to help us distinguish between things. The name neither has the same value as the thing named nor does it have the same function. For example, let me demonstrate by using the name or the label we use to identify the fruit we call "apple." By just saying the name of the fruit no one, not even in the slightest, would know how delicious an apple is. Only when we put an apple in our mouths and taste the apple do we begin to understand what an apple tastes like and can begin to understand the sensation of "delicious." Let me use the names of people as another example. My name is Kyoshin Asano. The character for Asano is made up of two Chinese characters. The first is the character "*asa*" which means "shallow." It is the antonym for the word "deep." The second character of my name or "*no*" is the character used to describe a field found in a valley. If you were to ask, "Does this mean that you are a shallow field as opposed to a deep field?" I would have to answer that there is absolutely no connection between me and the meaning of my name. Asano is simply my family name. It is a convention used to distinguish my family from others. If you were to continue with the same line of inquiry and ask me about my first name, which means "to have faith in the teachings," you might similarly assume that I was a very smart person based on the meaning of my name. But, this is not a valid conclusion. I am not at all an intelligent person. From these examples, we come to understand that the titles or names that we use to label things do not really describe, at all, the thing that it labels.

The Name Namo Amida Butsu, however, is different. This is because the Name arose after Amida Buddha put all of the Buddha's virtues into the Name. This name functions in accordance with the virtues of Amida Buddha.

Thus, if we were to repeat the Name in accordance with the desire of the Primal Vow, the virtues of the Name become the virtues of the person repeating the Name. Because of this, we are able to reach the level of Buddha-hood with just the *voiced utterance of the Nenbutsu*. Here, the *voiced utterance of Nenbutsu* is the *easy practice*. However, the *voiced utterance of Nenbutsu* is also said to have superior virtues (value). The reasons given for its superiority are also the reasons why Shinran Shonin threw away the practices of Mount Hiei, and why he chose the path of the *voiced utterance of Nenbutsu*. It is because he chose this path of the Nenbutsu that for the first time he was able to gain the promise of becoming a Buddha even while being in a confused human state. He was able to declare that he had discovered himself in the place of *total assurance*.

Going to be Born After Receiving Namo Amida Butsu—The Birth of Going Through Faith

The world of *total assurance* that Shinran Shonin was able to experience is the world of Amida Buddha's salvation. That it was possible to reach this world of *total assurance* through the voiced utterance of Namo Amida Butsu is recorded in the work by Shinran Shonin titled the "Meaning of the Passages on the Single and Many Thought Moments." In this work, Shinran Shonin writes:

"The way of Jodo Shinshu is the *going to be born through the Nenbutsu*."

Moreover, in examining how this was something that was transmitted to Shinran Shonin through Honen Shonin, we are able to see how the *going to be born through Nenbutsu* has the three major unique characteristics of simplicity, universality and superiority.

Having inherited this teaching of *going to be born through the Nenbutsu*, Shinran Shonin, who gained the state of *total assurance*, also used a completely different expression to describe this world. This expression is found within the Shonin's most important writing or "Passages on the Teaching, Practice and Enlightenment That Reveal the Truth and Reality of the Pure Land[8]." In the beginning of the first chapter or the Chapter on Teaching is expressed:

> "As I carefully consider this Jodo Shinshu there are two kinds of *merit transference*. The first is the *form of going*. The second is the *form of returning*. With regards to the *merit transference of the form of going* there is the True and Real Teaching, Practice and Enlightenment."

These words express the way the Shonin understood the salvation of Amida Buddha. This understanding is referred to as "*the birth of going through Faith*" or again as "*the path of uniquely achieving with just faith.*" Both of these terms try to express the uniqueness of Amida Buddha's salvation. In other words, the salvation of Amida Buddha —namely the point in time when the "*Faith*" that is transferred is received—occurs when the state of *total assurance* is opened up. On this point we are able to reach the exact same result by saying the Name of Amida Buddha or the *going to be born through Nenbutsu*.

Going to be born through Nenbutsu and *going to be born through Faith*

As written previously, because Shinran Shonin received the ideas of Honen Shonin the *birth of going through Nenbutsu* that was emphasized by Honen Shonin is acknowledged as adequately exhibiting the uniqueness of Amida Buddha's salvation. However, if we were to state why Shinran Shonin chose to use the expression *going to be born through Faith* instead, it is because a possible ambiguity can be found in expressing the salvation of Amida Buddha through saying the Name or *going to be born through Nenbutsu*. This ambiguity is one where even while we are repeating the Name of Amida Buddha we still cannot rule out the possibility that the utterances are no more than an imitation of the Nenbutsu. Imitating the Nenbutsu is not much different from deliberately choosing not to say the Buddha's Name because we are fearful of looking bad in front of people. Imitating the Nenbutsu is just an outward and insincere expression. It is something that can be uttered even if our true appreciation of the Nenbutsu is the complete opposite of what is being expressed and can be used to hide our true intent. Yet again there is the opposite case where we come to believe that within our very earnest action of uttering (the Name) that there is some kind of power to be found in those utterances. Each of these examples is contrary to the temperament that should be found in the correct activity of *going to be born into the Pure Land*. However, if we were to judge from outward appearances alone it is not possible to distinguish between those who have veered away from the Nenbutsu that is the correct activity for *going to be born* from those who have not. From this fact the difficulty that arises is that we have to become aware that a huge difference exists between these two acts even while we assume the same outward appearance. Shinran Shonin through clarifying the point where this difference occurs made clear the distinction between the true and the assumed Nenbutsu that comes from uttering the Buddha's Name with our mouths. At the same time, he also clearly indicated which of these two distinct approaches towards Nenbutsu would bear fruit.

Now, returning to describe the characteristics of *going to be born through Nenbutsu* that was emphasized by Honen Shonin, we gave the three points of (1) simplicity, (2) universality and (3) superiority (the *Name that bestows all virtues*). This Nenbutsu is the heart of the Buddha that tries to have us stand within the state of *total assurance*. When we receive the Buddha's heart just as it is we utter Namo Amida Butsu from our mouths. Because the *Power of the Buddha* (the Power of the Other) wants to save *sentient beings* and has becomes the *Name-and-Title* (the Buddha's Name), the optimal way to affirm that it has been received is through the action (*karmic action*) of *praising* (*saying*) *the Name*. Again, this form also expresses the unique feature of Amida Buddha's salvation. *Saying the Name* is already something that has been selected by the Buddha (*to select*) and was fulfilled by the Buddha. In other words, within the forty-eight vows that clearly indicates the Buddha's heart, the Eighteenth Vow (the Primal Vow) states:

"If, when I become a Buddha, the people of the worlds in the ten directions, from a *true heart* have *joyous faith* (have faith), and desire to be born in my country *with even ten thoughts* are not able to be born there, then I will not take true awakening..."(my personal interpretive reading)

The expression "*with even ten thoughts*" clearly expresses the selection and fulfillment of the Name. Although saying the Name of Amida Buddha with our mouths is something that we do as part of our actions, being able to *go to be born into the Pure Land* through *saying the Name* is completely due to the Power of Amida Buddha. This is called the *Nenbutsu of Other-power*.

What we have to be careful about here is that with regards to Honen Shonin he understood the Primal Vow in terms of our saying the Name of Amida Buddha as an action that befits the Primal Vow. As such, this act is something that complies with the Primal Vow. This action is the correct *causal property* that allows us to be born in the Pure Land. This is the assertion of *Nenbutsu is primary*. This kind of expression or "*Nenbutsu is primary*" is based on the traditional Buddhist perspective of emphasizing practice. It was also used to counter the argument that we cannot discuss something that is not related to the Buddhist Path. Furthermore, in discussing how the Nenbutsu compared with other aspects of the Buddhist Path that heretofore made practice central, it was probably thought convenient to talk about the practice of saying the Name. By doing this, Nenbutsu had the same quality as other practices (and the discussion would become a comparison between different practices). The reason this is important is because now the attributes of the Nenbutsu practice or simplicity, universality and superiority could be instantly identified.

Shinran Shonin naturally acknowledged that the *voiced utterance of Nenbutsu* that was emphasized by Honen Shonin made birth in the Pure Land possible because it is in accordance with the Buddha's Vow and that it is not voiced in order to accumulate merits through our own efforts. However, although there is no mistake in saying that *repeating the Name* is the correct action that leads to birth in the Pure Land instantly, in contrast to Honen Shonin, Shinran Shonin emphasized the point that for someone to manifest the *saying of the Name* with their voice they had to first receive in their heart the salvation of Amida Buddha. Within this heart that has accepted Amida Buddha's salvation is the manifestation of the voiced Namo Amida Butsu. Here, Shinran Shonin did not see the action associated with the true cause of birth in the Pure Land just in terms of the voiced Name and instead saw the true cause of birth in the Pure Land as being the heart that accepts and receives salvation. This is called *going to be born through Faith* or the heart that accepts Amida

Buddha's salvation. In other words, the emphasis is placed on *Faith* as the true cause for birth in the Pure Land.

Shinran Shonin's understanding of the Primal Vow

As written previously, Shinran Shonin, while inheriting Honen Shonin's *going to be born through Nenbutsu*, clearly indicates that the source of that Nenbutsu, from our perspective, can be found in the heart that has faith in Amida Buddha. Moreover, the Shonin's emphasis of *going to be born through Faith* is not an arbitrary, independent conclusion, but is founded on the explications found in the Sutra as well as the tradition established through the understanding of the Seven Masters[9]. In particular, with regards to what is explicated in the Sutra, the Eighteenth Vow that is shown in the Larger Sutra (the foundational Sutra that explains the salvation of Amida Buddha) was deeply investigated and the *true cause* for birth in the Pure Land was shown to be *Faith*. In other words, in the following section of Primal Vow where it states

"the people of the worlds in the ten-directions, from a *true heart*, having *joyous faith* and a desire to be born in my country"

the heart of the Nenbutsu follower is described through the three hearts of "*true heart*," "*joyous faith*," and "a desire to be born in my country (the *heart that desires for birth*)." The Shonin saw that it is these three hearts in particular that describes the heart of the person who has received the salvation of Amida Buddha. The *voiced utterance of the Name* was seen as the manifestation of this heart through our voices. Moreover, he also made it clear that these three hearts are unified by the heart found in the middle or "*joyous faith*" and indicated that in particular *joyous faith* is the *true and real Faith*. In other words, the Shonin stated that it is the *joyous faith* in particular that most appropriately reveals the condition of the heart that has received Amida Buddha's heart. He further states that the essence of *joyous faith* is the *true heart* and that the remaining *heart that desires for birth* is the desire that is found within *joyous faith*. Adding a little more explanation, the *true heart* refers to the point where the true and real heart of the Buddha that is trying to save us reaches us. This true and real heart becomes the heart that takes refuge in the Buddha's salvation and is called *joyous faith*. Although it is obvious that we have yet to reach the Buddha's country, this *joyous faith* continues to reside within our hearts. Within this heart that expresses our having taken refuge, the heart that desires for birth or the heart that understands that there is no mistake that we will be born in the Buddha's country is found. For this reason, the two hearts found before and after is included within and forms the *joyous faith*. In this way the contents of *Faith* is made clear.

In the general public there are instances when we use words such as *"true heart"* or "true and real heart" to express the condition of our hearts when it is serious and sincere. However, if we were to really look at the nature of our own hearts we would discover that in reality our hearts lack both durability and universality. Instead of "truth" we find that our hearts are often filled with emptiness and nonsense. If anything, we would find that our hearts lack truth. In the things that we do, for example, has there been anyone who has actually accomplished something to its ultimate conclusion? However, if the Buddha's true and real heart has been received, because this is the real thing, it is not something that we can manipulate as we wish. If we were to ask, "How is this true and real heart delivered to us?" we discover that it is because the Buddha has already fulfilled this heart for us and directly gives it to us (*transference of merit*) that we are able to receive it. In order to make this point clear Shinran Shonin changes the reading of the passage found in the Larger Sutra that indicates the fulfillment of the Primal Vow (*the passage on fulfillment*) and writes:

> "All the various peoples give rise to the heart of faith upon hearing the reason for the *Name-and-Title*. If one is able to rejoice with at least a single thought, <u>because this is given from the Buddha's *true heart*,</u> if one desires to be born in the Buddha's Country you will be established with the body that can immediately go to be born." (author's rendering)

Within this passage, in the part that is underlined, the normal reading is, "with a *true heart* one *transfers*," and has the meaning of "the person who wants to go to be born *transfers*[10] with a *true heart*." Instead, this part is being read, "with a *true heart* it is being given" and the action is one where we are receiving from the Buddha's *true heart* that is doing the giving. Moreover, if we were to look at the words prior to the underlined passage, the Shonin gives particular attention to the phrase "upon hearing the reason for the *Name-and-Title*," and through this makes clear that it is from the Buddha's *true heart* that the Buddha's *Name-and-Title* is being directed towards us.

Here the path of salvation of *going to be born through Faith* that is indicated by Shinran Shonin becomes clear. That is, even within the passages from the Chapter on Teaching that were given earlier or:

"with regards to the *merit transference of going* there is the true and real Teaching, Practice and Enlightenment"

the perspective of the Shonin is straightforwardly indicated. In other words, what is known as the *form of going* is expressed in the term *"the form of going to be born into the Pure Land."* The Shonin informs us that the *form of our going to be born* into the Pure Land of Amida is expressed in the four steps of teaching (that which is indicated in the Larger Sutra of Immeasurable Life), Practice (the salvation that is directed towards us from within the Buddha's *Name-and-Title*), faith (the *joyous faith* that is found in our taking refuge in the *Name-and-Title* of the Buddha that is also the activity of the Buddha's salvation) and Enlightenment (the result that is gained through *joyous faith*). Each of these, however, is clearly indicated as due to the working of the Buddha and is directed or *transferred* to us. Within the *Faith* that receives this *transference* from the Buddha is where the path of *going to be born into the Pure Land* is opened. It is also here where the remarkableness of the Shonin can be found.

The Nature of Faith

The aspects of *Faith*

While looking at the differences in expression between Honen Shonin and Shinran Shonin, we discover that the world of *total assurance* that Shinran Shonin was able to reach is the world of *Faith*. This world of *Faith* is the world where we take refuge in the work of salvation by Amida Buddha. Upon receiving this world of *Faith*, our actual human lives move towards the future life. In other words, instead of reaching the empty world that comes because of death— or what is considered to be the conclusion of human life—it is said that we go to the world of Amida Buddha where a wonderful life unfolds. Moreover, this *Faith* that is given to us through Amida

Buddha is where the outstanding feature of Jodo Shinshu's theory of salvation is found.

Next, while touching on the points made above, I would like to elucidate upon the world that opens up because of having received this salvation.

Making evident the circumstances of how salvation is fulfilled for us—through using the four points of teaching, practice, faith and enlightenment—Shinran Shonin delineates for us how our salvation can be found at the moment of faith (where *joyous faith* is *Faith*). Moreover, if we were to indicate what this faith is by describing the condition found within our hearts, it would be the state where our hearts are completely reliant upon Amida Buddha or the Buddha who is trying to save us. Using Shinran Shonin's words it is the state where, "*the cover of doubt is not mixed in.*" The *cover of doubt* is the harboring of doubt in our hearts. It is giving rise to doubts relative to the salvation of Amida Buddha who, in trying to save us, works to save us by becoming the *Name-and-Title* that is Namo Amida Butsu. Again, in contrast to Honen Shonin who explained the salvation of Amida Buddha in terms of being saved through saying Namo Amida Butsu, what is called the *cover of doubt* includes such things as harboring the doubt of whether or not I can be saved through such a simple means, or again if we are preoccupied by our own faults or bad karma, then it would also include making haphazard conjectures such as the following: Can someone like myself be saved? Even assuming that I can be saved, because it probably requires actions that can eliminate bad karma, and even if Namo Amida Butsu can become that action, wouldn't it require many utterances? This is what is called the *cover of doubt*[11].

Calling the contents of faith the lack of doubt in our hearts is, put in a different way, saying that faith is the condition where we have taken refuge in the *Name-and-Title* of Amida Buddha or the working of the Buddha's salvation. In other words, it is to be in harmony with the activity that is demonstrated through the *Name-and-Title*. Therefore, in order to be saved by Amida Buddha all we have to do is receive the working of the *Name-and-Title*. This alone is sufficient. Other than this—for example having to be in a convenient location, having to be at a particular time, having to have the correct attitude, having to accumulate merits, having to have life experiences or a salvation that would tend to exclude the young, and having to confess to all of our sins—there is not a single condition necessary for us to meet. Conversely, if you feel that there is some condition that needs to be met, then you will not be within the salvation of Amida Buddha. This condition of not having the *cover of doubt being mixed in* also describes the emotional state of absolute reliance. Because this emotional state is what it means to be secure within the Buddha's salvation, this too also describes the *heart of assurance*.

The faith that is *transferred*

When we find spiritual peace within the Buddha's salvation the Buddha's heart naturally enters and fills us resulting in our being able to be born into Amida Buddha's world. Saying this another way, the faith that establishes our birth in Amida Buddha's world is the point of contact where we can step into the unlimited world that is different qualitatively to our limited existential reality. We are also able to live within this unlimited world at the moment of faith, and when life comes to an end we are able to become completely without limits.

This qualitative transformation from the limited to the unlimited through faith is not something that we—who are limited—can gain from our side. Without receiving the work from the unlimited this qualitative transformation is not possible. For this reason, as written earlier, the *Faith* that resides in Amida Buddha's salvation is, in reality, the arrival of Amida Buddha's salvation within us. According to the Shonin this *Faith* is something that is conferred by (given from or *transferred* by) the Buddha. It is because it is *transferred* by the Buddha that a limited being can gain entry into an unlimited world. Here, it can be said that the salvation of Jodo Shinshu, as opened up by the Shonin, was accomplished through the theory of *transference* or the theory of the *transference of the Buddha's Vow power*.

In this way, once the establishment of the moment of salvation has passed, the activity of that salvation then manifests itself as the *voiced utterance of the Name* or Namo Amida Butsu. This *voiced utterance of the Name*, Namo Amida Butsu, is the same as that of Honen Shonin who said that all you have to do is utter the Name and you will be saved. For this reason, the *going to be born through Faith* as indicated by Shinran Shonin is something that we can understand as a clear explanation as to why Honen Shonin would encourage the *voiced utterance of the Name* that is filled with virtues, easy to utter and is superior. Thus, the perspective of Honen Shonin who encouraged only the *voiced utterance of the Name* can be said to be the *voiced utterance of the Name* that has this *Faith* within it, as was elucidated by Shinran Shonin, but was not something that was brought to the foreground by Honen Shonin.

The simplicity and transcendental superiority of *going to be born through Faith*

It can probably be said that the reason why the Shonin placed the point of *establishing the birth of going* at the moment that the faith that is *transferred by the Buddha* is received is because he wanted to make those characteristics that Honen Shonin identified as the unique features of the salvation that comes from *saying the Name*—simplicity, superiority, universality, and its aspect of being true and real—easier to understand. In other words, according to Honen Shonin, because the *voiced utterance of the Name* or Namo Amida Butsu is something that is easily repeated from anyone's mouth it is the *easy practice* (easily performed act) and is called this in contrast to the superlative and difficult practices (the practices of the *gate of the path of* sages). Relative to this, if we are going to compare the *easy practice* nature of *going to be born through Faith* with the superlative and difficult practices, then what was made clear is how it was Amida Buddha that practiced the superlative and difficult practices that are necessary for a *sentient being* to become a Buddha and how this is *transferred* to *sentient beings* by becoming the Name-and-Title that is Namo Amida Butsu. This is where the *easy practice* nature is found. In other words, the merits that are necessary for we *sentient beings* to *fulfill Buddha-hood*, because it is all found without exception inside the Name-and-Title of Namo Amida Butsu, are no longer required for us to practice anew; it is here where the simplicity of the *voiced utterance of the Name* is found. Although it goes without saying that it is something that is easy for us to voice, more than this, however, becoming the Name-and-Title in this way —where the *easy practice* nature can be seen in how the practices for becoming a Buddha are contained within it—because the Name-and-Title is already within the faith that we have received, and because this means that the *easy practice* nature is already included, it can be said that there is nothing that can be an *easier practice* than this. Again with regards to its universality, it is the faith that is *transferred* (the faith conferred by the Buddha); because there is no other condition that is required, it has the attribute of being receivable by all people. This too is made clear.

Furthermore, with regards to faith's aspect of transcendent superiority, if we were to go through the arguments as written above, it becomes self-explanatory. In particular what has to be mentioned about the uniqueness of the Shonin's highly developed thesis is that it is faith that is directly connected to *achieving Buddha-hood* immediately. It is on this point that the transcendent superiority of Jodo Shinshu can be found. It is because of this that Jodo Shinshu can be considered one of the most highly developed of religions. On this point, in the next chapter, I would like to give a more detailed account of the *benefits* that accompany *Faith*. However, the transcendent superiority that is found at the point where faith is directly connected to *achieving Buddha-hood* is also where it is paired with its universality. If it was simply connected to *becoming a Buddha*, then the difficult practice that is known as the *gate of the path of sages* becomes the foundational principle. Based on this foundation the goal becomes the application or practice of the Buddhist Path. These schools of Buddhism that focus on this are known through such names as Tendai, Shingon and Zen; these schools are directly connected to *becoming a Buddha*. Their aim, however, is to achieve this status while in our current, mundane world. In the case of these various other schools of the *gate of the path of sages*, however, if you were to ask if anybody can achieve this ultimate goal of *becoming a Buddha*, then you would have to answer that this is not necessarily the case. Instead, only a limited number of individuals can achieve this. It can only be achieved by those individuals that can endure the practices set out by these various schools.

This salvation through faith that has been established by Jodo Shinshu differs from the path of *becoming a Buddha* through the *gate of the path of sages* that relies on the efficacy of the virtues gained by the practices done by the individual (*self-power*) and is the path of *becoming a Buddha* by wanting to become a Buddha through relying on the *power of the Buddha*: these two paths differ in where they are grounded. Furthermore, this point of difference is also where the universality of Jodo Shinshu can be found. Because this universal aspect is also said to be founded on our human natures, as long as this universal aspect continues to exist (or how anyone can receive salvation), and because this is where becoming a Buddha is directly connected, we can say that the transcendent superiority of Jodo Shinshu's salvation through faith is made clear.

One aspect that is revealed through the faith that is *transferred*—the nature of *criminal evil being deep and heavy*

What has been written previously is the unique characteristic of the path of *becoming a Buddha* through the *faith transferred by the Buddha*. Although this can be viewed from various perspectives, we were exploring the unique characteristic of what it was that Shinran Shonin received through his experiences while he was aiming towards the ultimate goal of Buddha-hood. In contrast to this, one more unique characteristic that must be included can be explored through what can be called the rear view. This is something that becomes clear when we consider the various necessary causes for Amida Buddha to have become a Buddha and why the virtues thus gained were *transferred* to us.

Originally, the Pure Land Teaching is the path of wanting to *achieve Buddha-hood* through going to be born into the Pure Land of Amida Buddha with the desire of becoming a Buddha. This, it goes without saying, is the teaching of Sakyamuni—although it arose as an *explanation of the Dharma while considering the person being taught*—that from a historical perspective was proposed in terms of being a practice of the Buddha Path or as something that required actual doing. In other words, through practice, or doing those things necessary to become a Buddha, human beings began to awaken to their innate lack of ability. Realizing or fulfilling this potential of practice—the cause for becoming a Buddha—became a burden for those who could not reach the final goal. In other words, the ultimate desire of those people to *become a Buddha* could not be fulfilled through the practices that were used to become a Buddha. For those who could only dream of achieving Buddha-hood there grew a need to reconsider the path of *becoming a Buddha*. This reconsideration came after having to acknowledge their lack of ability: this is the source for the historical development of the Pure Land Path. In this way, seeing things from a historical perspective, the inherent inability of human beings to become a Buddha, which came together with the realization of the hypocrisies found within our human natures, gradually deepened until it became understood as the construct of human evil. This new construct or understanding led people such as Zendo Daishi[12] from China to go so far as to write such things as:

"I, as manifested, (am) a *foolish being of criminal evil and of birth-and-death* who from *vast kalpa* (past) to this moment have been constantly sinking and constantly sent adrift; there is no condition for my leaving and distancing myself from this."

In this statement we can reasonably say that, temporally speaking, the idea of personal evil has been deepened to its ultimate expression. In this expression, those who have this nature of *criminal evil* have confirmed the existence of the *path to becoming a Buddha* through vocalizing the Buddha Name of Amida Buddha as the cause for achieving the *fulfillment of the Buddha-path*.

This, in Shinran Shonin, is expressed as:

"The entirety of the *ocean of the multitudes*, from the beginning-less past to the present, to the present day, to the present moment, as those who are *sullied in evil, soiled and stained* do not have a pure heart...(they) do not have the heart that is true and real."

As can be found in this expression, beyond the deepening of the sense of a personal evil from the temporal perspective, Shinran Shonin has through expressions like "the entirety of the *ocean of the multitudes*" has deepened the idea of human evil to include the evil found inherent in all living things. Here, regardless of whether or not the ultimate desire for humans to *become a Buddha* is present, he sees this goal as destined for failure and has awakened to the powerlessness of humanity itself. This human that is good for nothing, the path for this person to *become a Buddha* can be none other than through the faith that is *transferred* by the Buddha.

In other words, the under-side that has been indicated through this *faith that has been transferred* is the *ultimate evil* nature of humans. Moreover, because it is this *faith that has been transferred by the Buddha* that can render humans—those who hold this *ultimate evil*—into truth and reality itself, that Shinshu is said to be the teaching that aims to save especially the evil person (the *evil person as the true object of salvation*). It is here that the origins of this teaching can be found. Truly, we should recognize deeply our true self.

3 *THE CRIMINALLY EVIL* NATURE OF HUMANS

Criminal Evil as Found in Morality

The uniqueness of the salvation of Amida Buddha that was revealed by Shinran Shonin, in other words the salvation of Shinshu, can be seen in how it is found at the point where the faith that is *transferred* by the working of Amida Buddha himself is received. It is here—how it can be received by anyone—where its universality and simplicity, as well as the pure aspect of *Other-power* can be seen. On the other hand, however, it is also through this faith that is *transferred* that the unique characteristic of our *criminal evil* nature as human beings is being forcibly proposed.

Next, let us explore deeply the matter of this *criminal evil* nature. Although the term *criminal evil* is a word that can be communicated with meaning in our general, daily lives it is a term that began as two separate terms: "criminal" and "evil." Evil is a word that is contrasted with "good." It is a term that means, "a bad thing" or "something that lacks truth." Criminality is a term that points to such things as: (a) actions or errors made in opposition to that which is considered moral, (b) that which is held in aversion by people such as defilements and disasters, (c) crime, and (d) actions that are contrary to the doctrine of Buddhism or Christianity. In these definitions the term "criminality" talks about human actions whereas the term "evil" has a slightly different nuance. However, when it becomes a compound term, the term *"criminal evil,"* more or less, becomes restricted to human actions and is generally used to mean "actions contrary to morality."

The kinds of actions that can break the associations between people is something that we hope to be able to eliminate through our own efforts. More than just hope, however, we also believe that this state is possible for us to achieve. That our everyday lives are based on this foundation is probably not something that needs to be restated now. When these acts become habituated, or becomes a part of our everyday lives, we find that we are able to maintain these acts without too much trouble. It becomes part of our daily routine. It is only when we meet with people in a new circumstance that we falter and experience discomfort.

For this reason, the *criminal evil* found in the world of morality, because it is something that destroys the world of morality, is something that needs to be eliminated. We can probably also say that it is something that has the characteristic of that which can be eliminated.

The Criminal Evil of Buddhism

Next, the *criminal evil* of the religious world is also something that destroys. It is something that can destroy the religious world and because of this, in order to reach the religious world, is something that needs to be eliminated. It is also something that has the attribute of potentially being eliminated. If we were to speak in terms of general Buddhism, it is that which keeps us from reaching the world of Enlightenment or the goal of all those on the Buddhist path. It is just that the term *criminal evil* is not used. Of course, within the old scriptures, although the term evil is used as in "Not doing the various evil acts, performing good, making your heart pure: this is the teaching of the Buddhas" (from the Lotus Sutra), the compound term *criminal evil* is not found. The term that is generally used in Buddhism to describe that which can prevent someone from reaching the world of Enlightenment is *"confused"* (*ignorance, passion*). Our actions, because they are confused, act against Enlightenment.

Although these acts can be seen as those acts that destroy Enlightenment, in the ultimate sense these acts are not seen as things that can infringe upon Enlightenment. In other words, according to Buddhism, that which can prevent Enlightenment is the status of our hearts or that which gives rise to and is the source of our actions. The status of our hearts is ultimately what is being addressed. The status of our hearts is what is said to be *confused* (delusional, uncertain, that which does not have correct wisdom, *passion*). It is said that what is representative of this heart of ours is the *three poisons of passion* or greed, anger and stupidity.

In this way, the heart of *passion* regulates our actions (the three karmic acts of body, mouth and mind) that occur in our daily lives. It is our hearts that make our daily actions go counter to Enlightenment. It does so to the point where, in the end, we would even ignore our morality and even commit acts that will destroy our morality. Furthermore, this condition of our hearts, because these acts are all meant to simply satisfy the self, is a very concrete way of showing how we are attached to the self (*self-attachment*). Even if we were really thinking of benefiting another person and did one thing for them, at the base of this is hidden the thought, "As long as it benefits me." For this reason, *passion* is called *criminal evil* and from the perspective of the Buddha's purity would have to be described as a defilement or as an impurity.

The realm of Enlightenment of the Buddha, the world where this kind of *passion* is extinguished (the world of nirvana), is a place that is filled with the Buddha's heart of great compassion. In other words, in order to reach the world of the Buddha, all we have to do is perform rigorous practices and through these practices eliminate *passion*. Thus, according to general Buddhism, or the teachings to reach the world of the Buddha from the world of our reality, it is through doing practices, while in our reality, and severing ourselves from *passion* that allows us to reach the goal of Enlightenment.

The Human Evil of Shinran Shonin

Eliminating *passion* as described previously is not an easy thing to do. Shinran Shonin who continued the practices of the Buddha Path for twenty odd years on Mount Hiei did so as a battle to eliminate this *passion*. If you were to ask if Shinran Shonin gained any benefit from doing these practices, then the answer would be, "No, he did not." Instead, it seems that the harder he tried to eliminate this *passion* the more it appeared. It came to the point where he could only admit that he was someone who was saturated by it. He recognized that even if he were to practice for an entire lifetime that he could not defeat this *passion*. This, we can say, indicated that he only existed as a being filled with *criminal evil* and that he could not eliminate this *passion* through his own power or abilities.

According to the typical way we live our lives within the world, although we continue to hold onto the *passion* of greed, anger and stupidity, having these attributes is seen as natural. We find little need to question this *passion*. Because of this, we also find no need to see these things as *criminal evil*. Furthermore, we seek our independence, we hope for peace, and we desire for equality. For the most part we feel that we have gained these things. However, if we were to consider it more carefully, then we would see the huge error we are making. For example, we humans see ourselves as being rational and conscientious. We see ourselves as being able to suppress the rampaging of our greed, anger and stupidity. From this the freedom, equality and peace that we have gained is based on the assumption that we can suppress these *three poisons of our passion*. Because of this, if our power to suppress is weakened, the *three poisons of passion* come to the fore and dance. We get stuck in a place from where we can no longer turn back. The rationality, conscientiousness and societal constraints that have the power to control are also only able to suppress our *passion* to a certain degree. When all is said and done all that is left is the world where our insatiable *passion*, filled with the three poisons, runs amok. For this reason, because we are filled with the *three poisons of passion* true freedom, true peace and true equality is unachievable. Only a limited freedom, peace and equality, found within our prejudices, is achievable. This is a pitiable and sad thing. Although it may be something we do not want to acknowledge, it is something that we must: this is who we are in the here and now.

Furthermore, as an example, even if we were to examine what is known as the three primary instincts of humankind—the desire to live, the desire to eat and the desire to procreate—or those qualities that are inherent in the *passion of greed*, we come to understand how each of these is also replete with the nature of *criminal evil*. Within these three primary instincts, the core can be found in the desire to live. It can be said that the desire to eat is the way the desire to live manifests itself in a particular person as something to fulfill independently, and that the desire to procreate is an aspect of the desire to live that is manifested as the preservation from one person to the next. What then is this desire to live? Although it is not really something that needs to be expressed anew, I would like to re-examine this topic again from the point of view I am now exploring.

The desire to live is the power that attempts to maintain the life of a single individual. Those entities that have life on this planet include both plants and animals. Plants in general, we can claim, are able to continue and maintain their lives without sacrifice of other lives. On the other hand, and in particular with human beings, the life of any particular person is maintained only through the sacrifice of other lives. Taking the life of another is how our lives are maintained. We will go as far as it takes, even if it means taking another life, to enrich this single life of ours. This attribute of self-enrichment that is a part of the desire to live is also something that is typically not self-aware. In other words, unconsciously we hold onto the idea that it does not matter how our life is preserved so long as we are able to maintain it. Because the conditions for our preserving our lives is more or less met within our daily lives, we tend not to recognize its existence and bury it within our unconscious. If we were to take an example from the animal-world, what would happen if there was a great famine? The strong would kill and eat the weak. We hear and see this often. Although this is frightening to admit, we human beings, each and every one of us, also have this unconscious desire to live. Furthermore, if this desire to live has been able to maintain itself from the very first appearance of humankind until the present, then this is something that could cause our hairs to stand in fright. All of us, regardless of who it might be, as a matter of course, have this desire to live. In fact, because this is something that is so natural for us to have that we are able to maintain and preserve this desire to live while typically being completely and mindlessly ignorant of our having this desire. Again, what should we say to the fact that we do not refer to this desire to live as *criminal evil* and instead just ignore its existence? Although it is sad to admit, as a human being is it simply okay for us to shrug our shoulders and say, "This is just something that cannot be helped?"

This way of seeing how, from its very beginning, humankind has been filled with this *passion* and seeing this as our identity is expressed by the Chinese Master Zendo Daishi who says:

"I, as manifested, (am) a *foolish being that is (filled with the) criminal evil of birth-and-death* who from vast *kalpa* (past) to this moment has been constantly sinking and constantly sent adrift; there is no condition for my leaving and distancing myself from this."

Shinran Shonin expresses the same thought as:

"All those found in the ocean of the masses, from the past that has no beginning to this day, to this moment being sullied in defiled evil do not have a heart of purity…(and) do not have the heart that is true and real."

Therefore, the self-awareness of human evil that can be seen here is not simply what is mundanely called guilt but is the sense of our *criminal evil* (guilt) that is shown to us as we stand before the Buddha. Furthermore, if it is something that is difficult to see through our personal abilities alone, then it also becomes something that only a Buddha can eliminate. It is here that we should probably deeply reflect on the uncompromising yet trustworthy salvation of Shinshu that was elucidated to us by the Shonin.

4 THE BENEFIT OF FAITH, PART 1

The Benefit of Going to be Born is Becoming a Buddha (Future Benefit)

In the previous section I considered the ultimate evil nature—the *criminal evil* nature—of human beings as seen through the *three poisons of our passion* and through our desire to maintain life. This *criminal evil* nature was introduced as something that is revealed to us as one aspect of the faith that is *transferred*. However, this *criminal evil* was also described as one of those things that we human beings overlook as a matter of course. I think that it has also been made clear that this is one point where we greatly or perhaps more accurately fundamentally need to rethink our human existence.

In talking about what kind of benefits are gained through the salvation that comes with the *Faith* that is given (*transferred*) by the Buddha, because this is something that I have written about previously in the chapter where I talked about the "Distinctive Features of Jodo Shinshu" and give "The salvation of *going to be born is becoming a Buddha*" as one of those distinctive features there may not be a need to talk about this topic again. On the other hand, however, as a *benefit* of faith "The salvation of *going to be born is becoming a Buddha*" is something that cannot be overlooked from a global perspective. Although there will be places of repetition, because it is an important aspect of Jodo Shinshu I did not want to shy away from repeating myself.

With regards to this benefit of *Faith*, the first thing that needs to be written about is that we can achieve the Enlightenment of *going to be born is becoming a Buddha*. This Enlightenment of *going to be born is becoming a Buddha* is how, at the moment our actual lives come to an end, we go to be born into the Pure Land or the world of Amida Buddha. At the same time, at the moment we go to be born, we are able to become the same Buddha as Amida Buddha. Thus, this *benefit of going to be born is becoming a Buddha*, because it is the benefit gained at the time life in this world is exhausted, is the benefit of the world to come (future). It is called the *benefit to come* and is an expression used to describe one of the unique features found in the salvation of Jodo Shinshu.

The Pure Land as the World of Non-Regression

Next, if I were to explain why this future *benefit of going to be born is becoming a Buddha*—as a benefit of *Faith*—is a remarkable characteristic, it is because up until Jodo Shinshu, generally speaking, the Pure Land was, as the name suggests, "A Pure World." It is a world free of defilement and a world with a Buddha in residence. It is thought of as the ideal place to perform the practices of the Buddha Path. Why this is important is because the reality of our world is such that even if we were to practice the Buddha Path with devotion and were to demonstrate some positive result from that, various obstructions would arise and despite having made progress we would not see adequate enough results. The effect of that, in many cases, would be to make all of that practice moot. In other words, this world obstructs practice and we retreat back to where we started: the world, we can say, is filled with *conditions for regression*. For example, we can give the limitations of the human life-span as an instance of this. Even if we were to persevere for an entire life-time, with just fifty or sixty years of practice we would still be very far from reaching the Enlightenment of a Buddha. If we were to stop along the way to becoming a Buddha because of death, then the fifty or sixty years of accumulated practice would end in ruin. In contrast to this, the Pure Land or a land where a Buddha resides—being different from our world—is a world where the hindrances to practices do not exist. It is the world of *non-regression*. Because of this, all the positive results from our practice would manifest themselves one after the other. It is a world where we can finally achieve the Enlightenment of a Buddha; it is a world of purity. Thus, it goes without saying that those devotees of the Pure Land tradition would directly desire for birth in the Pure Land. Even those of the *gate of the path of sages* who hope to achieve the Enlightenment of the Buddha through their *self-power*, have desired to be born into this kind of Pure Land and in that Pure Land continue to persevere in their practice to achieve the Enlightenment of a Buddha.

In this way, although we are ultimately able to achieve the Enlightenment of a Buddha in this kind of a Pure Land, the Pure Land itself is seen as a place conducive to practice. Because of this, in the case of a person trying to achieve the Enlightenment of a Buddha through *self-power*, this person has to continue to perform the practice that was done in this world. For this person, as long as it is a Pure Land, it probably does not matter which Buddha's Pure Land it is. Moreover, for this person to achieve the Enlightenment of a Buddha the length of time necessary to become a Buddha is said to be *three asogi*[13] *hundred great kalpa*. We need to accumulate practices over a long, unfathomable period of time. Although I just mentioned that the period of practice will be for a long unfathomable period of time, because it is still not clear how long this is let me add a few words of explanation. A *kalpa* is a unit of time used to describe a long indeterminate period. Also, because it is a unit meant to describe a long length of time that cannot adequately be described by numbers it can only be expressed by way of an example. These examples include the story of the boulder *kalpa* and the story of the poppy seed *kalpa*. Using the explanation of the boulder *kalpa* found in the Sutra on the Establishing Acts of the Bodhisattva Necklace we are told that there is a great stone with sides forty *li* (157.08 km) in each direction. Once every three years a heavenly being comes down from the heavens and with a robe of feathers weighing three *shu* (2.01 g) wipes the stone with the ends of the robe. In the amount of time it would take for this stone to be completely ground away by the sleeves of this heavenly being is roughly the length of one *kalpa*. Hopefully, through this analogy, we get a better idea of how hard it is to become a Buddha through the practice of *self-power*.

Desiring the *birth of going* to the Pure Land as a place of practice means that even if we were able to achieve birth in the Pure Land we would still, over a very, very long period of time, have to continue to accumulate practices. At the end of this process, we would finally be able to reach the Enlightenment of the Buddha. In review, the Pure Land is a world without the *conditions for regression*: there is no returning again to a world filled with *conditions for regression* regardless of however long the period of time may be. Because of this, there is no deviating from the true path and mistakenly going onto a different one. As a unique characteristic of the Pure Land we can give the trait of it being a place where we can absolutely open the doors to Enlightenment. For this reason a person who was able to be born into the Pure Land is referred to as someone who *resides within the gathering of the rightly established*. What it means to *reside within the gathering of the rightly established* is to become a member of those individuals or the gathering of those who are set to truly become a Buddha. Regardless of however long the period to become a Buddha may be, receiving this status is regarded as something that cannot be more desirous.

Again, these kinds of practices exercised over a long period of time in the Pure Land are also done to collect the virtues that are worthy of a Buddha. This would include all those *internal* virtues such as the *four wisdoms*[14], the three bodies[15], the ten powers[16] and the four strengths[17] as well as all the *external* virtues such as *desirous attributes*[18], *illuminating light*[19], *giving discourse*[20], and *giving benefits*[21]. In order to accomplish this, the fulfillment of Buddha-hood, we would need to accumulate these virtues from innumerable practices that have at their center the six practice methodology of giving, maintaining precepts, having forbearance, persevering, having calm settlement, and having wisdom[22].

The General Causal Law of Going to be Born Into the World of Non-Regression

Although the Pure Land is a splendid world where all the effort exerted to perform the practices leading to Buddha-hood do not go to waste, the Pure Land itself is a difficult place to get to. Looking at the explanations found in the Sutra, in order to be born into this place of practice you need to become a Buddhist Priest in the world of the here and now and exercise various virtues; if you are unable to become a priest, then you will need to exercise various good deeds, maintain purity, build pagodas and Buddha statues, give offering to priests, adorn the altar before a Buddha, and continue to worship. Moreover, until you die and with singleness of heart that does not waiver, these activities must never be interrupted. When your life comes to an end in this world, if a Buddha does not come to receive you, then you are still not able to *go to be born* into the Pure Land.

Because of this, even if the Pure Land is the perfect place for practice if the manner of your practice in the here and now is bad, then, although it goes without saying, even if you were to put everything you had into your practice in both body and spirit, if a Buddha does not come to receive you then you are not able to be born into the Pure Land. For this reason you cannot, even for a moment, allow your heart any laxity; until the very last moment of your life, the very last instant, you simply have to fervently endeavor with everything riding on your desire for birth. Under these circumstances, it is almost impossible to have the confidence to feel that everything is okay and that I can go to be born. Furthermore, even with regards to the way you persevere there is neither a limit saying that this is good enough, nor is there any guarantee. Because of this, even while practice with an *unwavering singleness of heart* is ceaselessly demanded, within the shadow of practice follows the uncertainty of, "Is this good enough?" If you were to show any kind of uncertainty on your face, then you have already shown that you did not have the *unwavering singleness of heart* sufficient for birth. Already the failure of practice is born; conversely, this also means that the hope of *going to be born into the Pure Land* cannot be fulfilled. Because this kind of practice is filled with so much distress, it is called the *path of difficult practice*.

The Pure Land that is the World of Going to be Born is Becoming a Buddha

The *benefit* due to faith that was made clear by Shinran Shonin, because he definitely talks about *going to be born* into the splendid and quiescent world of the Pure Land of Amida Buddha, is as written previously achieving birth into a world that does not have any conditions for regression. However, the *birth of going* that comes from the benefit of faith that is *transferred by the Buddha* does not simply talk about being born into the Pure Land of Amida Buddha that has no condition for regression but, together with this birth, also talks about becoming the same Buddha as Amida Buddha. From the previous perspective, or the idea where you can only become a Buddha after being born into the Pure Land and then only after a long period of practice following that birth, the benefit due to faith that was revealed by the Shonin, because you are now able to become a Buddha immediately at the same time you *go to be born*, the meaning of *going to be born* becomes different. It comes to have the meaning of being able to observe the splendor of becoming a Buddha without the movement of time.

If we were to consider things from the perspective of having to continue practice even after being born in the Pure Land, then the idea of instantly becoming a Buddha at the moment we *go to be born* as a benefit of faith will probably be seen as a disregard for practice and as absurd. However, it is here that the unique characteristic of the benefit of faith that is *transferred* can be found. It is also here, found within Faith, where the reason why it has to be this way can be found. In other words, although it is something that I have already written about, the reason that we can become a Buddha at the same time we go to be born is found within the *transferred* faith that is received from the Buddha.

This faith that is *transferred*, because it arises due to Namo Amida Butsu—the Name-and-Title that is the working of Amida Buddha's salvation—is the faith that entrusts in the Name-and-Title and has within it all the virtues found within the Name-and-Title; this is what is bestowed. Accordingly, this faith that is *transferred* is something that holds the same virtues as the Name-and-Title, and because of this if we were to elucidate the virtues that are held by the Name-and-Title, this point becomes clear. In other words, within the Name-and-Title, within the person who has taken refuge in Amida Buddha, is bestowed the benefit of the virtue known as *going to be born is becoming a Buddha*; this is encompassed as the benefit of faith. Moreover, the Buddha who fulfilled this Name-and-Title that has within it this kind of virtue, regardless of how numerous Buddha who have established a Pure Land may be, is Amida Buddha alone. It is for this reason that those who have received the *transferred* faith that is the salvation of

Amida Buddha are bestowed the virtue of the *benefit of going to be born is becoming a Buddha* as the benefit of faith. It is here that there was special reason to make a note of this.

As mentioned previously, because becoming a Buddha means becoming a Buddha identical to Amida Buddha, those who go to be born are immediately able to work or operate in a manner identical to that of Amida Buddha. This activity of saving *sentient beings* is known as the work of *the form of returning*. In other words, returning once again back to the world of confusion we are able to do the work of saving *sentient beings* who are easily confused.

The above is the benefit that comes from the faith that is bestowed. If we were to indicate this in terms of the relationship of *cause and effect* because faith is the cause, *going to be born is becoming a Buddha* is the effect. This relationship has, from the past, been given as a unique characteristic of Jodo Shinshu's understanding of the *effect that is Enlightenment*[23].

5 THE BENEFIT OF FAITH, PART 2

The Fulfillment of Karma in the Present

We were able to see how through the receipt of the faith that comes from the Buddha, how at the moment life in this world comes to an end, that we are able to *go to be born* into Amida Buddha's world and simultaneously gain the benefit of achieving the same Enlightenment as that of Amida Buddha. There is, however, one more benefit. This too is something that requires special mention. Let us consider this other benefit.

Through the faith that is received as the salvation of Amida Buddha, although the *benefit of going to be born is becoming a Buddha* is guaranteed at the same time that the irrefutable end of our lives come, when this faith is received it is also realized within our daily lives and not just at the time of the end of life. Accordingly, because the *benefit that will come* is determined, the work of receiving the great benefit that is known as *going to be born* is fulfilled in the present life (within our daily lives). With this meaning the term *"The fulfillment of karma in the present"* is used. This is another unique characteristic of the faith of Jodo Shinshu. This is a unique characteristic of Jodo Shinshu because the conventional understanding of the Pure Land teaching uses terms like *coming to receive at the expected end* (death) or the *fulfillment of karma at the expected end* instead. In other words, even while anticipating the salvation of Amida Buddha the *voiced utterance of the Nenbutsu* is continued until life comes to an end and it is only at that moment, when life comes to an end, that—for the first time—birth in the Pure Land becomes clear. For this reason, within the various *annuls on the birth of going* (records of people who have *gone to be born*) written during the Heian period of Japan the circumstances of the end of life are painstakingly recorded. In these annuls it is recorded that in order to gain proof or to find assurance that someone was indeed going to the Pure Land a string was placed from the person's hand who is dying to the hand of the Buddha statue that was placed at the head of the pillow. In Japan, using the Buddha's *pictographic image in the role of coming to receive* those who were dying saw particular development as a technique used to gain proof that a person had *gone to be born* at the moment of death. Because of this, the unique trait of Shinran Shonin's Faith characterized by the *fulfillment of karma in the present* has to be seen as a great distinction.

Even Honen Shonin, Shinran Shonin's teacher, seemed to think that whether or not we can be born into the Pure Land would finally become clear at the moment we anticipate our death. However, we also come to understand that because of the way that Honen Shonin thought about the approach of death, his understanding was quite different from that of the general Pure Land teachings. Honen Shonin's understanding was the same as Shinran Shonin. In other words, although generally the anticipation of death is seen as something extending beyond the time of ordinary life, the thinking of Honen Shonin was that there is no established period that can be called ordinary life. As found in the statement, "If the anticipation of death is extended, it is ordinary life; if ordinary life is shortened, it is the anticipation of death" we find in him no distinction between ordinary life and the anticipation of death. This way of thinking by Honen Shonin, at first glance, appears difficult to comprehend. If we think carefully on the matter, however, because we cannot anticipate when the approach of the end (death) will come, the breath we take in becomes the end of life; the breath we expel, that moment, also becomes the end of life. We can say, then, that human life itself is the compilation of the end of many lives. On this point, Honen Shonin understood how important each and every moment of ordinary life is through the form of anticipating the end.

Now, with regards to Shinran Shonin, although the expression may be different, because he indicates clearly that the proof of the salvation of Amida Buddha is found in faith he has inherited the thinking of Honen Shonin. However, we come to understand that in doing this, he has rejected the generally accepted understanding of the anticipation of the end as the moment of proof and is strongly bringing to the forefront the aspect of Amida Buddha's salvation in the here and now.

The Ten Kinds of Benefits in the Present Life

As written above, in that moment in our daily life when we receive faith the promise of the ultimate objective of Buddhist practice that is known as *becoming a Buddha at the moment one goes to be born* is guaranteed. This was examined through the aspect of *the fulfillment of karma in the present*. It is here that we are able to see how Shinran Shonin tried to affirmatively grasp human life in the here and now. In other words, we come to understand that Shinran Shonin made clear the path of achieving the ideal of Buddha-hood while living life as a layperson. Of course, although Honen Shonin also did not negate the perspective of the lay person and worked diligently towards its affirmation, we are not able to see the same force as that found in Shinran Shonin's affirmation.

Although the Shonin's understanding is founded on the perspective of Honen Shonin, even in looking at what he said regarding the fulfillment of the *karma for the birth of going* (*fulfillment of karmic circumstances*), Honen Shonin's perspective would be one where each and every *voiced utterance of the Name* is said at the anticipation of death and the accumulation of these utterances is where human life is realized: we are given a pressing feeling of the tragic beauty that stops our breath. However, the *fulfillment of karmic circumstances* of Shinran Shonin that comes from his understanding of faith is something that informs us instead of the assurance that can be had. In particular, the Shonin, in addition to the *future benefit* that comes with this understanding of faith or *becoming a Buddha at the moment one goes to be born*, is able to express the ten kinds of benefits in the present that is received by the person of faith. While this is something that should probably be taken up as its own subject, it is here that the pressing feeling that makes you want to stop your breath disappears. Rather, we are able to feel a sense of overflowing and relaxed relief.

If we were to explain what these ten kinds of benefits that we receive in the present lifetime are they would be the following:

1. The *benefit of being protected and held by those multitudes unseen*: the benefit of being protected through the powers of the Buddha, Bodhisattva and other deities that we cannot see with our eyes.
2. The *benefit of consummating the supreme virtue*: the benefit of having received the unsurpassed virtue, or receiving the value of becoming a Buddha.
3. The *benefit of transforming evil and becoming good*: the benefit of having evil turned into good.
4. The *benefit of being protected and thought of by the various Buddha*: the benefit of always being in the thoughts of the Buddha and being protected by them.
5. The *benefit of receiving praise from the various Buddha*: the benefit of being praised by all the Buddha.
6. The *benefit of constantly being protected by the heart's light*: the benefit of always being protected by the compassionate light of Amida Buddha's salvation.
7. The *benefit of having great joy in one's heart*: the benefit of always being able to live within joy.
8. The *benefit of understanding one's indebtedness and being able to respond to the virtues received*: the benefit of always understanding the indebtedness we have towards the Buddha and not being able to help ourselves from responding to that indebtedness.
9. The *benefit of constantly practicing great compassion*: the benefit of not being able to help ourselves from encouraging others to the Nenbutsu.
10. The *benefit of entering the ranks of the rightly established*: the benefit of having achieved the status of a person who will decidedly become a Buddha.

Although this is a list that indicates ten kinds of benefits, it is given as a representative list. Actually, immeasurable benefits are received. This list of ten is given because we cannot possibly record an immeasurable list one item at a time. Instead, it has been categorized concretely into these ten headings. If we were to look further at these ten kinds of benefits, we would find that they are not the sort of things that directly eliminate the inadequacies or the worries or the pains that are found in our daily lives. In other words, these are the benefits that we receive from a more fundamental perspective, one that is hidden behind the surface of our daily lives. For example, if we were to look at each of these ten individually, because the protection by the gods and Buddha is indicated, it is very easy to conclude that we will receive happiness right away. To be sure, although receiving the protection from the gods and Buddha will bring happiness, if that *happiness* is founded on individualistic wants and desires that are willfully selfish, then contrarily there is no protection from the gods and Buddha. That is to say, the gods and Buddha do not protect in order to create a self-serving happiness. Rather, admonishing people from holding such willfully selfish views is the real protection that the gods and Buddha provide. The reason for this is because the primary source from which the benefits are given is the Vow of the Buddha to have us live a true and real life found within truth and reality. Through these ten kinds of benefits we are again made to become aware of our lives in a more fundamental and essential way. We are being helped to see our lives more completely.

The Benefit of Entering the Ranks of the Rightly Established

Within these ten benefits, the tenth or *entering the ranks of the rightly established* is one that summarizes the other nine kinds of benefits; the other nine kinds of benefits reveal the contents of the *benefit of entering the ranks of the rightly established*. For this reason, the summarization of the immeasurable virtues that are bestowed in the present life is the *benefit of entering the ranks of the rightly established*. The benefit that comes in the here and now of Jodo Shinshu is exhaustively expressed through the *benefit of entering the ranks of the rightly established* or to reach the status of having our future Buddha-hood established. Moreover, this benefit—as can be seen through its contents—is the same as the contents of faith itself. It is here that the uniqueness of Jodo Shinshu's benefit that comes in the here and now can be seen.

In other words, from the general perspective of practicing the Buddhist Path this "status of having established becoming a Buddha" is, as it is in Jodo Shinshu, called the level of *having entered the ranks of the rightly established.* Also, because there is no such thing as returning to confusion upon achieving this status, meaning that you will not revert back to a confused state, it is also called the status of *non-retrogression.* Within the stages of practice of the Buddhist Path that are divided into fifty-two levels before achieving Buddha-hood, this is equivalent to the forty-first step; it refers to the *first level of being grounded* of the *ten levels of being grounded* of the Mahayana Bodhisattva (or the ten levels of the Bodhisattva)[24]. It is also seen as corresponding to the level that a person who achieves birth in the world of a Buddha or a Pure Land attains. What this is saying is that because there is nothing to interfere with practice, because there is no condition that can cause regression in a Pure Land, this is birth into a world of *non-regression.* Since this is the case, we also achieve the status of *ranking with the rightly established.* Thus, in order to reach the status of *ranking with the rightly established,* practice that is appropriate to reaching that level is necessary; it is not something that you can arrive at readily. In other words it is not the kind of status that you can achieve without being the possessor of exceptionally superior attributes.

In this way, what was considered having achieved an extremely high status in general Buddhism or entry into the *ranks of the rightly established,* is now in Jodo Shinshu considered a benefit that is spontaneously received in the present life as part of the faith that is given to us from the Buddha. Furthermore, even while we may not be endowed with any attribute of particular merit, we can within our lives in the here and now receive Amida Buddha's salvation and because of this we have, at the same time, reached the status of having secured Buddha-hood or having reached the *ranks of the rightly established.* We can say that this is the greatest of benefits possible. If I were to add my thoughts to this, then if we were to try to gain birth in Amida Buddha's Pure Land like we try to do in Shinshu but attempt to do so through the efforts of the practice prescribed by general Buddhism, then regardless of how diligent we may be in our practice the proof that we are able to be born through the efficacy of that practice cannot credibly be found until the very last moment of our lives. Because of this, those who attempt this are, as a matter of course, not permitted to live their days haphazardly. But, even if their practice is done with diligence, there is no conclusive evidence that the practice they have done is ever enough. If, in the worst case scenario, their heart becomes confused at the very last moment of life, all the practice that was done at the risk of their lives, like a bubble, and in a glimmer, will end in vain. Moreover, regardless of who it may be, if a human being is not able to reach the final moment of their own life with confidence then how pitiful, and how unreliable that life is. You cannot help but to give a long sigh at this kind of existence. In contrast to this, however, the benefit of *entering into the ranks of the rightly established* that is found in Jodo Shinshu in the present life is something that we have to consider as something truly remarkable.

The Same as Maitreya, Being Similar to the Buddha

If we were to rely on the salvation of Amida Buddha, then within the faith that allows us to receive the Buddha's activity of salvation we are able to establish our status as a person who will absolutely become a Buddha at the same time life comes to an end. Therefore, there is no necessity to wait for the moment of death's approach. Instead, regardless of when life might come to its end there is no need to worry at all. For this reason, because we are made to become a Buddha at the same time this human lifetime ends, we are able to wait and anticipate this final moment with joy. From this meaning of indicating that becoming a Buddha is established, becoming someone who is among the *ranks of the rightly established* is also described as *"being like the Buddha," "subsequently being the same as Maitreya"* or as *"the rank of being similar to one truly awakened."* These descriptions are all expressing the magnificence of this benefit. In other words, *entering the ranks of the rightly established* is to be placed at that level of *being similar to one truly awakened* or the ultimate level of the Bodhisattva which, generally speaking, is not something that we can hope to achieve. Instead we become the same as Maitreya Bodhisattva or the Bodhisattva who has achieved the ultimate status of the Bodhisattva. All this is placed within the moment of faith.

"Being similar to one truly awakened" is the fifty-first rank of the fifty-two levels of practice along the Buddhist Path (ten levels of faith, ten levels of residence, ten levels of practice, ten levels of transference, ten levels of being grounded, the *level of being similar to awakening* or the *level of being similar to one truly awakened*, and the *level of wondrous awakening* or the *level of the Buddha*). The level of *being similar to one truly*

awakened is one just prior to the *level of wondrous awakening (level of Buddha-hood)* and because it is similar to *true awakening (wondrous awakening)* it indicates the stage before *wondrous awakening* is opened. Currently, the activity of Amida Buddha's salvation that has been received by those of the Nenbutsu is one where, together with the end of life, you gain the exact same Enlightenment as that of Amida Buddha *(level of wondrous awakening)*. At the same time we receive the working of salvation the same Enlightenment as that of the Buddha is promised from the side of the Buddha. Because we are within the *ranks of the rightly established* this is something that would correspond with the rank that is the equivalent to the *level of being similar to Enlightenment (similar to true awakening)* which, in terms of practice along the Buddha path, is just before the *level of wondrous Enlightenment*. For this reason the receipt of faith is also called *"reaching the level of being similar to true awakening."* Again, with the same meaning, it is also called *subsequently being the same as Maitreya* and *thus being the same as Maitreya*. These terms are in praise of the virtues of the person of Faith. The expression *subsequently being the same as Maitreya* has the meaning of being the same rank as that of Maitreya Bodhisattva and is also expressed as *thus being the same as Maitreya* (that is, to be the same as Maitreya). Maitreya Bodhisattva, through the *self-power* practices of the Buddhist Path, is a Bodhisattva who has already achieved the *level of being similar to Enlightenment*. Following Sakyamuni Buddha's entrance into nirvana, our world or the Saha[25] world of suffering became a world without a Buddha. Although Maitreya is a Bodhisattva that will appear in the future (after 5,670,000,000 years) and become a Buddha to save *sentient beings*, from the meaning of filling the space left behind by a Buddha he is also called *Maitreya that fills the place of a Buddha*. This Maitreya Bodhisattva has the rank of *being similar to one truly awakened* which is just one step before the ultimate level of Buddha-hood. The person who has received the salvation of Amida Buddha, the person of *Faith*, is also just a step away from opening up to the same awakening as Amida Buddha. Because both Maitreya and the person of *Faith* are at the same level of being just a step before Enlightenment, although the virtues that come from *self-power* and the virtues that come from *Other-power* are different, from the perspective that both have reached the point just before awakening the person of *Faith* is praised as *thus being the same as Maitreya, subsequently being the same as Maitreya* or again as having reached the level of *being similar to true awakening*.

In particular, Maitreya Bodhisattva, who is deeply revered as the future Buddha, has reached the level of *being similar to true awakening* which is the ultimate level achievable through *self-power* practice. There are even Sutra that describe this Bodhisattva becoming a Buddha and from old the worship of Maitreya Bodhisattva has flourished. In this way, because Maitreya Bodhisattva has reached the status of becoming a Buddha in the future, there is also the aspect of Maitreya being worshiped as Maitreya the Buddha even in the present. From this meaning, because the person of *Faith* will open up to the same awakening as that of Amida Buddha after their life comes to an end, the virtues of the person of *Faith* is praised by referring to that person as *"being similar to the Buddha."* Here, the world of *Faith* that receives the salvation of Amida Buddha has the meaning of being completely resolute. It is here that the human life that cannot end in futile emptiness appears.

The Ten Benefits in the Present Life (Part 1)

What I have been writing about until now has been the general examination of the ten kinds of actual benefits that are received when we rely on the working of Amida Buddha's salvation (*Faith*). In particular, because the *"benefit of entering into the ranks of the rightly established,"* the tenth of the list of benefits, summarizes the entire group it was written that this benefit also describes the unique characteristic of the way Shinshu looks at benefits in general. Next, I would like to spend some time talking about the other nine benefits in a little more detail.

Upon looking at the first nine benefits, benefits one through six all describe something that moves towards us from the outside and is not something that we can directly see or touch. The last three benefits of this list or *having great joy in one's heart, understanding one's indebtedness and being able to respond to the virtues received,* and *constantly practicing great compassion* all appear within our daily lives. In other words, the first six benefits talk about the virtues found within *Faith* and are not something that can be clearly shown in concrete form in our daily lives.

Although a distinction is made between the multitudes unseen (gods of heaven, gods of earth and the like) and the various Buddha

(Buddha other than Amida Buddha), benefit number one and number four or *being protected and held by those multitudes unseen* and *being protected and thought of by the various Buddha* both talk about how the person of Nenbutsu is protected. Here, what is expressed by being protected is the protection of our adamantine *Faith*. This meaning is different from the typical worldly expression of our asking for protection by the various gods and Buddha. In other words, when we see the word "protection" we quickly think of things like being protected from the suffering that comes from the loss of such things as financial stability. To be protected from the financial challenges that we face in our daily lives we hope for protection in the form of wealth. We think of being freed from the suffering of illness and the suffering that accompanies materialistic considerations. We ask to be protected in the form of having good health and having a lifestyle that is abundant in material things. We think of being protected so that we can be complimented on the amount of intelligence that we have and hope that it is not lacking. We also think of being protected so that we do not meet with things like traffic accidents. These are the sort of things that we tend to think of as the distinctive characteristics of the workings of the gods and Buddha in protecting us. However, this kind of protection is a misunderstanding of the true meaning of what a god or a Buddha is. In other words, although these are weaknesses that we human beings tend to have, they are also problems that we can find solutions to by simply applying some effort on our own part and not trying to find an easy and effortless solution. Understanding what it means to be protected by the gods and Buddha in this way is completely self-serving and lacks self sufficiency. Asking for the protection by the gods and Buddha in this way is selfish. It is nothing more than trying to prop up one defective part of our life. In contrast to this, although it goes without saying that it also deals directly with the way we live our lives, Shinshu does not try to fix any particular aspect of our lives. At the same time, however, Shinshu is also not talking about something that a human being can achieve just by trying hard enough. What it is referring to is the resolution of the fundamental human problem, the problem that we as human beings have to settle so long as we are human, and at the same time is also something that we cannot resolve, regardless of how much effort we put into it, because we are human. It is talking about the resolution of death. It is talking about protecting the Faith that is the resolution to this fundamental dilemma. It is here that the true and real form of the protection by the Buddha and gods can be found. In other words, the true meaning of being protected by the Buddha and gods is found in the resolution of *birth-and-death*.

The second benefit of *consummating the supreme virtue* is the benefit of having the ultimate and supreme virtue given to us. The normal virtues that we amass during our daily lives is a piecemeal type of virtue and because of this can never become an ultimate virtue. What is meant by supreme virtue is the *Name-and-Title* of Amida Buddha itself (because it was mentioned earlier that the *Name-and-Title* of Amida Buddha has within it all the countless virtues, I will not include a detailed description here). Expressed differently, while the virtues that we are able to achieve are piecemeal, we discover that they also lack durability. On the other hand, the *Name-and-Title* of Amida Buddha has within it all the various virtues as well as having the quality of durability. It does not matter when or where or what the situation may be, these virtues will not be compromised. They will not change. For this reason it is called the ultimate and supreme virtue. It is because it is this kind of virtue that it is able to resolve the fundamental problem of *birth-and-death* that we humans are not able to resolve.

Moreover, the third benefit of *transforming evil and creating good*, although we must taste the pains of the world because we exist as the *criminally evil filled with birth-and-death*, tells us that through the salvation of Amida Buddha the highest and ultimate virtue replaces *criminal evil*, and that because of this we are able to distance ourselves from the world of suffering and have it transformed into good. What is meant by the terms evil and good here, although it does include the meanings found in their general, common usage, is something a little more fundamental in its meaning. In other words, it is referring to the fact that human beings are existences that necessarily must perish while constantly repeating the cycle of *birth-and-death*. This fact, itself, is being regarded as evil. Of course, included within this is the evil that is spoken of in general or the evil that runs contrary to such things as morality and the law.

However, the evil that is spoken of generally, because it is an evil that is superficial and transitory, can be atoned for and these acts can be expunged. The evil of *birth-and-death*, on the other hand, is not something that we can abolish with our own power. Because the world misunderstands this, the world believes that even the moral and legal meaning is immutable. For example, let us say that a person commits the crime of second degree murder and is punished with fifteen years of hard labor. After serving the sentence of hard labor, although restitution for the crime should have been paid after the fifteen years, this person will have to live as a criminal with the previous conviction of murder until he dies. Even after his death the family will be shunned as a murderer's family. Although this might be the real punishment for the crime of murder, even if the individual might still be classified as a criminal while serving the sentence, after having served the sentence for the crime, because restitution for the crime was made through serving the sentence, that individual should have been returned to the state of a true human being from that of a criminal. That this person has a criminal record is, to the contrary, something that has to be considered as committing the error of changing something that is temporary and discontinuous and making it into something permanent. That is to say, while we outwardly use beautiful expressions like, "hate the crime, not the person" to describe the transitory nature of crime, in the end we do hate the person. In making this shift it is only we humans that commit the crime of *birth-and-death*. Moreover, because *birth-and-death* is something that cannot be erased throughout eternity, it becomes something that we need to bear and show repentance.

Next, the fifth benefit of *receiving praise from the various Buddha* is the benefit where the various Buddha praise those people who have gained *Faith* by saying things such as, "This is my very good friend," or "This person is a White Lotus among people," or "This is a person of superior understanding far and wide," or "This is a person of great dignity and virtue." In other words, our relying upon Amida Buddha, because it is to know the meaning of the true human life, is the reason why the various Buddha would praise us. Stated differently, we can say that the various Buddha calling us, "My very good friend" exists to help us understand the true human life.

Next, the sixth benefit of *constantly being protected by the heart's light* refers to the light of Amida Buddha's salvation that is constantly protecting the person of *Faith*. That is, Amida Buddha will protect the true and real *Faith* of the person of the Nenbutsu until the moment of life's end, or the moment we become a Buddha. Because of this, the heart's light is "Amida Buddha's heart's light." This is an expression that helps to describe the activity of salvation of the Buddha and should be understood to mean that the Buddha's activity of salvation is constant.

The above benefits from the first or *being protected and held by the multitudes unseen* to number six or *constantly being protected by the heart's light* all describe the benefits that are given to us from the outside. The meaning that these virtues have, we should not forget, also has within them the unique contents of Shinshu.

The Ten Benefits in the Present Life (Part 2)

Next, regarding the final three benefits of the first nine, although the first six cannot be seen with our eyes, these benefits come from without and indicate that benefits naturally appear in our daily lives.

First, the seventh or the benefit of *having great joy in one's heart* tells us that within the heart of the person who relies upon Amida Buddha is a heart filled with joy. Even while appearing that we have heard and understood the words of Shinshu, in reality, because we infrequently find ourselves staring into the true depths of *birth-and-death* within our own existence, many feel apprehension or insecurity towards their reliance upon Amida Buddha. This is because even as they understand salvation the joy from that salvation does not really arise. Of course, although there is no error in this kind of understanding, this is being pointed out because it is different from the kind of true and real reliance that Shinran Shonin was able to reach. Because our understanding tends to be scholastic we stand upon that precipice. When our hearing the Dharma and experience deepens (although this deepening is as varied as there are people and no single account can be established) from the depths of our own heart the thing we call *birth-and-death* is acknowledged as "that single great thing" in our personal lives. It is at this time that this seventh benefit or the *having great joy in one's heart* is gained. However, even if we do not go that far, as our intellectual understanding of Amida Buddha's salvation progresses, our understanding will have advanced to the extent that there is no comparison to the time when we did not know what salvation was and our feelings of joy towards things will become greater. For example, the settlement of the single great thing in life is not something achievable through our own power. When we realize that the only way to do this is through the power of Amida Buddha we come to know of the tireless and exhaustive efforts of Amida Buddha to reach us. If we were to give the death of another person as an example, then as we are confronted with the experience of the death of others it is through the deepening of that experience that the acknowledgment of "the single great thing" is gradually deepened; the settlement of this experience that comes with receiving faith is what becomes joy.

Next is the eighth benefit or *understanding one's indebtedness and being able to respond to the virtues received.* This is the virtue where the person who relies upon Amida Buddha is constantly able to feel indebtedness towards the salvation of Amida Buddha and is, furthermore, able to repay that indebtedness. This benefit is something that physically occurs within our daily lives. Describing this through Shinran Shonin's words he says, "Simply and constantly praise the Tathagata's (Buddha's) Name and repay the indebtedness towards the great compassion, the widely promised Vow." As stated in the passage, praising the *Name-and-Title* of Amida Buddha with *Faith* is, in that act itself, knowing our indebtedness and repaying virtues. Why this is so is because praising the Name is itself the natural expression of having relied on Amida Buddha coming from our mouths. It is the concrete expression of the joy of having been saved and is, at the same time, the act of expressing our gratitude. On the other hand, what we need to be careful about is, while it is not something that is pushed onto others, because it is the act of repaying the indebtedness that comes from having been saved by the Tathagata it also must become the act that comes from the feeling of needing to share this with others.

The next or the ninth *benefit of constantly practicing great compassion* is the benefit of being able to always perform the same work as that found in the Buddha's compassion. Being able to perform the same work as Amida Buddha's compassion is, although it is not impossible to interpret this to mean that we can save other people as freely as Amida Buddha can, in the Shonin's words:

"Why is this called Great Compassion? If we were to continue the Nenbutsu exclusively without stop, following that moment of life's end, we then establish our birth into *assurance and bliss.* If we can hurriedly encourage each other in the practice of Nenbutsu, all this is called the person who completely practices *great compassion.*"

As can be seen in these words, being able to encourage another person to become a person who says the Nenbutsu is to practice *great compassion*. As also can be seen through this passage, like the eighth benefit of *understanding one's indebtedness and being able to respond to the virtues received*, this benefit is centered around the Nenbutsu. Speaking from a slightly broader perspective, this can also be understood to mean that any action that facilitates the gaining of faith can all be considered the practice of *great compassion*. Moreover, this is not something done from time to time, but is constant. For this reason, caution must be taken to emphasize the point that this is not done only when the mood arises.

In this way we come to know that the final three benefits of the first nine benefits are those that express themselves in our reality. Those that feel pride in being aware of the salvation of Amida Buddha, at the same time they feel the joy of knowing that these benefits exist, cannot help but to feel penitent over their imperfections. In this way we come to know that the salvation of Jodo Shinshu lies within gratitude and penitence.

Appendix

Alphabetical Listing of Translated Technical Terms (Part 1)

achieve Buddha-hood	成仏 (jou-butsu)
achieving Buddha-hood	成仏 (jou-butsu)
animal	畜生 (chiku-shou)
attached	執着 (shuu-jaku)
awakened person	覚者 (kaku-sha)
becoming a Buddha	成仏 (jou-butsu)
birth-and-death	生死 (shou-ji)
birth-and-death is nirvana	生死即涅槃 (shou-ji-soku-ne-han)
Buddha	仏陀 (bud-da)
Buddha	仏 (butsu)
Chapter on Faith	信巻 (shin-kan)
Chapter on Practice	行巻 (gyou-kan)
emptiness	空虚 (kuu-ko)
empty	空虚 (kuu-ko)

empty existence	空虚 (kuu-ko)
entered through the gate (to become an initiate)	入門 (nyuu-mon)
entering the Buddhist Order	得度 (toku-do)
entering the priesthood	得度 (toku-do)
existence	有 (u)
heavenly beings	天 (ten)
hell	地獄 (ji-goku)
human beings	人 (nin)
hungry ghost	餓鬼 (ga-ki)
Hymns on the Masters	高僧和讃 (kou-sou-wa-san)
impermanence	無常 (mu-jou)
impermanent	無常 (mu-jou)
leaving the mundane world	出家 (shuk-ke)
left the mundane world	出家 (shuk-ke)

long night of birth-and-death, the	生死の長夜 (shou-ji-no-chou-ya)
Meaning of the Textual Passages on Only Having Faith	唯信鈔文意 (yui-shin-shou-mon-i)
Mount Hiei	比叡山 (hi-ei-zan)
nirvana	涅槃 (ne-han)
non-existence	無 (mu)
nothingness	無 (mu
ocean of birth-and-death, the	生死海 (shou-ji-kai)
ocean of suffering of birth-and-death	生死の苦海 (shou-ji-no-ku-kai)
ordination as an initiate into the Buddhist Order	得度 (toku-do)
Passages in Lament of Differences	歎異抄 (tan-i-shou)
path of achieving Buddha-hood	成仏道 (jou-butsu-dou)
path towards Buddha-hood	成仏道 (jou-butsu-dou)
self-attachment	我執 (ga-shuu)

six paths	六道 (roku-dou)
take the priesthood	得度 (toku-do)
transmigrating through the house of birth-and-death	生死輪転家 (shou-ji-rin-den-ge)
true tranquility	寂静 (jaku-jou)
Verses on the True Faith	正信偈 (shou-shin-ge)
warrior	修羅 (shu-ra)

Alphabetical Listing of Translated Technical Terms (Part 2)

abandoning the world	出家 (shuk-ke)
achieve Buddha-hood	成仏 (jou-butsu)
achieving the fulfillment of Buddha-hood	成仏 (jou-butsu)
Amida Buddha	阿弥陀仏 (a-mi-da-butsu)
annuls on the birth of going	往生伝 (ou-jou-den)
Ashuku Buddha	阿閦仏 (a-shuku-butsu)
assurance	安心 (an-jin)
assurance and bliss	安楽 (an-raku)
become a Buddha	成仏 (jou-butsu)
Becoming a Buddha at the moment one goes to be born	往生即成仏 (ou-jou-soku-jou-butsu)
becoming a Buddha with this body	現身即仏 (gen-shin-soku-butsu)
being similar to one truly awakened	等正覚 (tou-shou-kaku)

benefit of going to be born is becoming a Buddha, the	往生即成仏の利益 (ou-jou-soku-jou-butsu-no-ri-yaku)
benefit that will come	当益 (tou-yaku)
benefit to come	当益 (tou-yaku)
benefits	利益 (ri-yaku)
birth in the Pure Land	浄土往生 (jou-do-ou-jou)
birth into the Pure Land	往生浄土 (ou-jou-jou-do)
birth of going	往生 (ou-jou)
birth of going through Faith, the	信心往生 (shin-jin-ou-jou)
Buddha Path	仏道 (butsu-dou)
Buddha's efforts	仏力 (butsu-riki)
Buddha's power	仏力 (butsu-riki)
causal property	因法 (in-pou)
cause and effect	因果 (in-ga)
Chapter on Teaching	教巻 (kyou-kan)

coming to receive at the expected end	臨終来迎 (rin-juu-rai-kou)
comparison between different practices	行行相対 (gyou-gyou-sou-tai)
conditions for regression	退縁 (tai-en)
confused	惑 (waku)
cover of doubt	疑蓋 (gi-gai)
cover of doubt is not mixed in, the	疑蓋無雑 (gi-gai-mu-zou)
criminal(ly) evil	罪悪 (zai-aku)
criminally evil filled with birth-and-death	罪悪生死 (zai-aku-shou-ji)
desirous attributes	相好 (sou-gou)
Dharma body	法身 (hou-shin)
easy practice	易行 (i-gyou)
effect that is Enlightenment, the	証果 (shou-ka)
effort by the Buddha	仏力 (butsu-riki)

establishing the birth of going	往生決定 (ou-jou-ketsu-jou)
evil person as the true object (of salvation)	悪人正機 (aku-nin-shou-ki)
evil person as the true object of salvation	悪人正機の救い (aku-nin-shou-ki-no-sukui)
explanation of the Dharma while considering the person being taught	隋機説法 (zui-ki-sep-pou)
Faith	信心 (shin-jin)
faith that has been transferred by the Buddha	如来回向の信 (nyo-rai-e-kou-no-shin)
faith transferred by the Buddha	如来回向の信 (nyo-rai-e-kou-no-shin)
foolish being of criminal evil and of birth-and-death	罪悪生死の凡夫 (zai-aku-shou-ji-no-bon-bu)
foolish being that is (filled with the) criminal evil of birth-and-death	罪悪生死の凡夫 (zai-aku-shou-ji-no-bon-bu)
form of going	往相 (ou-sou)
form of returning, the	還相 (gen-sou)

four wisdoms	四智 (shi-chi)
fulfill Buddha-hood	成仏 (jou-butsu)
fulfillment of karma at the expected end	臨終業成 (rin-juu-gou-jou)
fulfillment of karma in the present, the	平生業成 (hei-sei-gou-jou)
fulfillment of karma in the present, the	平生業成 (hei-zei-gou-jou)
fulfillment of the Buddha-path	成仏道 (jou-butsu-dou)
future benefit	当益 (tou-yaku)
gate of the path of sages	聖道門 (shou-dou-mon)
gate of the Pure Land	浄土門 (jou-do-mon)
giving benefits	利生 (ri-shou)
giving discourse	説法 (sep-pou)
go and be born	往生 (ou-jou)
go to be born	往生 (ou-jou)
go to be born into the Pure Land	浄土往生 (jou-do-ou-jou)

going to be born	往生 (ou-jou)
going to be born in the Pure Land	浄土往生 (jou-do-ou-jou)
going to be born is becoming a Buddha	往生即成仏 (ou-jou-soku-jou-butsu)
going to be born is becoming a Buddha	往生即成仏 (ou-jou-soku-jou-butsu)
going to be born through Faith	信心往生 (shin-jin-ou-jou)
going to be born through the Nenbutsu	念仏往生 (nen-butsu-ou-jou)
great perfect mirror wisdom	大円鏡智 (dai-en-kyou-chi)
Great Teacher Shan Tao, the	善導大師 (zen-dou-dai-shi)
Great Teacher Tan Luan, the	曇鸞大師 (don-ran-dai-shi)
ignorance	無明 (mu-myou)
illuminating light	光明 (kou-myou)
joyous faith	信楽 (shin-gyou)
karmic action	行業 (gyou-gou)

Larger Sutra of Immeasurable Life	大無量寿経 (dai-mu-ryou-ju-kyou)
level of being similar to awakening	等覚位 (tou-kaku-i)
level of being similar to one truly awakened	等正覚位 (tou-shou-kaku-i)
level of the Buddha	仏位 (butsu-i)
level of wondrous awakening	妙覚位 (myou-kaku-i)
Maitreya that fills the place of a Buddha	補処の弥勒 (fu-sho-no-mi-roku)
Meaning of the Text on the Single and Many Thought Moments	一念多念文意 (ichi-nen-ta-nen-mon-i)
Meditation Master Tao Cho, the	道綽禅師 (dou-shaku-zen-ji)
meditative retreat	参籠 (san-rou)
merit transference	回向 (e-kou)
merit transference of the form of going	往相回向 (ou-sou-e-kou)
Mount Hiei	比叡山 (hi-ei-zan)

Nagarjuna Bodhisattva	龍樹菩薩 (ryuu-ju-bo-satsu)
Name	御名 (mi-na)
Name that bestows all virtues	全徳施名 (zen-toku-se-myou)
Name-and-Title	名号 (myou-gou)
Nenbutsu is primary	念仏為本 (nen-butsu-i-hon)
Nenbutsu of contemplation	観念念仏 (kan-nen-nen-butsu)
non-regression	不退 (fu-tai)
non-regressive	不退 (fu-tai)
non-retrogression	不退転 (fu-tai-ten)
ocean of the multitudes	群生海 (gun-jou-kai)
Other-power	他力 (ta-riki)
Passages on the Teaching, Practice and Enlightenment That Reveal the Truth and Reality of the Pure Land	顕浄土真実教行証文類 (ken-jou-do-shin-jitsu-kyou-gyou-shou-mon-rui)
passion	煩悩 (bon-nou)

passion of greed	貪欲 (ton-yoku)
path of difficult practice	難行道 (nan-gyou-dou)
path of easy practice	易行道 (i-gyou-dou)
path of uniquely achieving with just faith, the	唯信独達の道 (yui-shin-doku-datsu-no-michi)
path to becoming a Buddha	成仏道 (jou-butsu-dou)
pictographic image in the role of coming to receive	来迎図 (rai-kou-zu)
power of the Buddha	仏力 (butsu-riki)
praising the Name	称名 (shou-myou)
Primal Vow	本願 (hon-gan)
Primal Vow of Other-Power	他力本願 (ta-riki-hon-gan)
Primary Scripture	本典 (hon-den)
Prince Regent Shotoku	聖徳太子 (shou-toku-tai-shi)
Pure Land	浄土 (jou-do)
reaching the level of being similar to true awakening	等正覚のくらいにつく (tou-shou-kaku-no-kurai-ni-tsuku)

recompense body	報身 (hou-jin)
Regal Priest Genshin, the	源信僧都 (gen-shin-sou-zu)
repeating the Name	称名 (shou-myou)
resides within the gathering of the rightly established	正定取に住す（る）(shou-jou-ju-ni-juu-su-ru)
responsive body	応身 (ou-jin)
retrogression	退転 (tai-ten)
Saha	娑婆 (sha-ba)
salvation by the transference of merit of Other-power	他力回向の救い (ta-riki-e-kou-no-sukui
salvation of Other-power	他力の救い (ta-riki-no-sukui)
salvation through the Other-power of the Primal Vow	他力本願の救い (ta-riki-hon-gan-no-sukui)
saying the Name	称名 (shou-myou)
self-attachment	我執 (ga-shuu)
self-power	自力 (ji-riki)

sentient beings	衆生 (shu-jou)
Seven Masters, the	七祖 (shichi-so)
six paramita	六波羅蜜 (rop-pa-ra-mitsu/roku-ha-ra-mitsu)
six perfections	六波羅蜜 (rop-pa-ra-mitsu/roku-ha-ra-mitsu)
soiled and stained	汚染 (wa-zen)
subsequently being the same as Maitreya	次如弥勒 (shi-nyo-mi-roku)
sullied in evil	穢悪 (e-aku)
sullied in evil, soiled and stained	穢悪汚染 (e-aku-wa-zen)
Sutra on the Establishing Acts of the Bodhisattva Necklace	菩薩瓔珞本業経 (bo-satsu-you-raku-hon-gou-kyou)
ten benefits in the present life	現生十益 (gen-shou-juu-yaku)
three asogi hundred great kalpa	三祇百大劫 (san-gi-hyaku-dai-kou)
three poisons of (our) passion	三毒の煩悩 (san-doku-no-bon-nou)

Three Pure Land Sutra	浄土三部経 (jou-do-san-bu-kyou)
thus being the same as Maitreya	便同弥勒 (ben-do-mi-roku)
to select	選択 (sen-jaku)
total assurance	安心 (an-jin)
transference	回向 (e-kou)
transference of merit	回向 (e-kou)
transference of the Buddha's Vow power	仏願力回向 (butsu-gan-riki-e-kou)
transferred	回向 (e-kou)
transferred by the Buddha	如来回向 (nyo-rai-e-kou)
transfers	回向 (e-kou)
transformative body	応身 (ou-jin)
true awakening	正覚 (shou-kaku)
true cause	正因 (shou-in)
true heart	至心 (shi-shin)

ultimate evil	極悪 (goku-aku)
unwavering singleness of heart	一心不乱 (is-shin-fu-ran)
various Buddha of the ten-directions	十方の諸仏 (jip-pou-no-sho-butsu)
vast kalpa	曠劫 (kou-gou)
Vasubandhu Bodhisattva	天親菩薩 (ten-jin-bo-satsu)
voiced utterance of (the) Nenbutsu	口称念仏 (ku-shou-nen-butsu)
voiced utterance of the Name	称名 (shou-myou)
wisdom of accomplishing metamorphosis	成所作智 (jou-sho-sa-chi)
wisdom of equality	平等性智 (byou-dou-sei-chi)
wisdom of wondrous perception	妙観察智 (myou-kan-zatsu-chi)
with even ten thoughts	乃至十念 (nai-shi-juu-nen)
wondrous awakening	妙覚 (myou-kaku)
worlds of the ten-directions	十方世界 (jip-pou-se-kai)

Alphabetical listing of Transliterated Technical Terms (Part 1)

a-shu-ra 阿修羅	*warrior*
bud-da 仏陀	Buddha
butsu 仏	Buddha
chiku-shou 畜生	*animal*
ga-ki 餓鬼	*hungry ghost*
ga-shuu 我執	*self-attachment*
gyou-kan 行巻	Chapter on Practice
hi-ei-zan 比叡山	Mount Hiei
jaku-jou 寂静	*true tranquility*
ji-goku 地獄	*hell*
jou-butsu 成仏	*achieving Buddha-hood, becoming a Buddha*
jou-butsu-dou 成仏道	*path of achieving Buddha-hood, path towards Buddha-hood*
kaku-sha 覚者	*awakened person*

kou-sou-wa-san 高僧和讃	Hymns on the Masters
kuu-ko 空虚	*emptiness, empty, empty existence*
mu 無	*non-existence, nothingness*
mu-jou 無常	*impermanence, impermanent*
ne-han 涅槃	nirvana
nin 人	*human beings*
nyuu-mon 入門	*entered through the gate (to become an initiate)*
rin-den 輪転	*transmigrating (through)*
rok-ka-ku-dou 六角堂	Rokkakudo (Hexagon Hall)
roku-dou 六道	*six-paths*
shin-kan 信巻	Chapter on Faith
shou-ji 生死	*birth-and-death*
shou-ji-kai 生死海	*ocean of birth-and-death*
shou-ji-no-chou-ya 生死の長夜	*long night of birth-and-death, the*

shou-ji-no-ku-kai 生死の苦海	*ocean of suffering of birth-and-death*
shou-ji-rin-den-ge 生死輪伝家	*transmigrating through the house of birth-and-death*
shou-ji-soku-ne-han 生死即涅槃	*birth-and-death is nirvana*
shou-ren-in 青蓮院	Shoren-in (Temple of the Blue Lotus)
shou-shin-ge 正信偈	Verses on the True Faith
shu-ra 修羅	*warrior*
shuk-ke 出家	*leaving the mundane world, left the mundane world*
shuu-jaku 執着	*attached*
tan-i-shou 歎異抄	Passages in Lament of Differences
ten 天	*heavenly beings*
toku-do 得度	*entering the Buddhist Order, entering the priesthood, ordination as an initiate into the Buddhist Order, take the priesthood*
u 有	*existence*

| yui-shin-shou-mon-i 唯信鈔文意 | Meaning of the Textual Passages on Only Having Faith |

Alphabetical listing of Transliterated Technical Terms (Part 2)

a-mi-da-butsu 阿弥陀仏	Amida Buddha
a-shuku-butsu 阿閦仏	Ashuku Buddha
aku-nin-shou-ki 悪人正機	*evil person as the true object*
aku-nin-shou-ki-no-sukui 悪人正機の救い	*evil person as the true object of salvation*
an-jin 安心	*assurance, total assurance*
an-raku 安楽	*assurance and bliss*
ben-do-mi-roku 便同弥勒	*thus being the same as Maitreya*
bo-satsu-you-raku-hon-gou-kyou 菩薩瓔珞本業経	Sutra on the Establishing Acts of the Bodhisattva Necklace
bon-nou 煩悩	*passion*
butsu-dou 仏道	Buddha path
butsu-gan-riki-e-kou 仏願力回向	*transference of the Buddha's Vow power*
butsu-i 仏位	*level of the Buddha*

butsu-riki 仏力	*Buddha's efforts, Buddha's power, effort by the Buddha, power of the Buddha*
dai-en-kyou-chi 大円鏡智	*great perfect mirror wisdom*
dai-mu-ryou-ju-kyou 大無量寿経	Larger Sutra of Immeasurable Life
don-ran-dai-shi 曇鸞大師	Great Teacher Tan Luan, the
dou-shaku-zen-ji 道綽禅師	Meditation Master Tao Cho, the
e-aku 穢悪	*sullied in evil*
e-aku-wa-zen 穢悪汚染	*sullied in evil, soiled and stained*
e-kou 回向	*merit transference, transference, transference of merit, transferred, transfers*
fu-sho-no-mi-roku 補処の弥勒	*Maitreya that fills the place of a Buddha*
fu-tai 不退	*non-regression, non-regressive*
fu-tai-ten 不退転	*non-retrogression*
ga-shuu 我執	*self-attachment*

gen-shin-soku-butsu 現身即仏	*becoming a Buddha with this body*
gen-shin-sou-zu 源信僧都	Regal Priest Genshin, the
gen-shou-juu-yaku 現生十益	*ten benefits in the present life*
gen-sou 還相	*form of returning, the*
gi-gai 疑蓋	*cover of doubt*
gi-gai-mu-zou 疑蓋無雑	*cover of doubt is not mixed in, the*
goku-aku 極悪	*ultimate evil*
gun-jou-kai 群生海	*ocean of the multitudes*
gyou-gou 行業	*karmic action*
gyou-gyou-sou-tai 行行相対	*comparison between different practices*
hei-zei-gou-jou 平生業成	*fulfillment of karma in the present, the*
hi-ei-zan 比叡山	Mount Hiei
hon-den 本典	Primary Scripture
hon-gan 本願	Primal Vow

hou-jin 報身	*recompense body*
hou-shin 法身	*Dharma body*
i-gyou 易行	*easy practice*
i-gyou-dou 易行道	*path of easy practice*
ichi-nen-ta-nen-mon-i 一念多念文意	Meaning of the Text on the Single and Many Thought Moments
in-ga 因果	*cause and effect*
in-pou 因法	*causal property*
is-shin-fu-ran 一心不乱	*unwavering singleness of heart*
ji-riki 自力	*self-power*
jip-pou-no-sho-butsu 十方の諸仏	*various Buddha of the ten-directions*
jou-butsu 成仏	*achieve Buddha-hood, achieving the fulfillment of Buddha-hood, become a Buddha, becoming a Buddha, fulfill Buddha-hood*

jou-butsu-dou 成仏道	*fulfillment of the Buddha-path, path to becoming a Buddha*
jou-do 浄土	Pure Land
jou-do-mon 浄土門	*gate of the Pure Land*
jou-do-ou-jou 浄土往生	*birth in the Pure Land, going to be born in the Pure Land, go to be born into the Pure Land*
jou-do-san-bu-kyou 浄土三部経	Three Pure Land Sutra
kan-nen-nen-butsu 観念念仏	*Nenbutsu of contemplation*
ken-jou-do-shin-jitsu-kyou-gyou-shou-mon-rui 顕浄土真実教行証文類	Passages on the Teaching, Practice and Enlightenment That Reveal the Truth and Reality of the Pure Land
kou-gou 曠劫	*vast kalpa*
kou-myou 光明	*illuminating light*
ku-shou-nen-butsu 口称念仏	*voiced utterance of (the) Nenbutsu*
kyou-kan 教巻	Chapter on Teaching
mi-na 御名	Name

mu-myou 無明	*ignorance*
myou-gou 名号	Name-and-Title
myou-kaku-i 妙覚位	*level of wondrous awakening*
nan-gyou-dou 難行道	*path of difficult practice*
nen-butsu-i-hon 念仏為本	*Nenbutsu is primary*
nen-butsu-ou-jou 念仏往生	*going to be born through the Nenbutsu*
nyo-rai-e-kou 如来回向	*transferred by the Buddha*
nyo-rai-e-kou-no-shin 如来回向の信	*faith that has been transferred by the Buddha, faith transferred by the Buddha*
ou-jin 応身	*responsive body, transformative body*
ou-jou 往生	*birth of going, go and be born, going to be born, go to be born*
ou-jou-den 往生伝	*annuls on the birth of going*
ou-jou-jou-do 往生浄土	*birth into the Pure Land*
ou-jou-ketsu-jou 往生決定	*establishing the birth of going*

ou-jou-soku-jou-butsu 往生即成仏	*becoming a Buddha at the moment one goes to be born, going to be born is becoming a Buddha*
ou-jou-soku-jou-butsu-no-ri-yaku 往生即成仏の利益	*benefit of going to be born is becoming a Buddha, the*
ou-sou 往相	*form of going*
ou-sou-e-kou 往相回向	*merit transference of the form of going*
rai-kou-zu 来迎図	*pictographic image in the role of coming to receive*
ri-shou 利生	*giving benefits*
ri-yaku 利益	*benefits*
rin-juu-gou-jou 臨終業成	*fulfillment of karma at the expected end*
rin-juu-rai-kou 臨終来迎	*coming to receive at the expected end*
roku-ha-ra-mitsu 六波羅蜜	*six paramita, six perfections*
ryuu-ju-bo-satsu 龍樹菩薩	Nagarjuna Bodhisattva
san-doku-no-bon-nou 三毒の煩悩	*three poisons of (our) passion*

san-gi-hyaku-dai-kou 三祇百大劫	*three asogi hundred great kalpa*
san-rou 参籠	*meditative retreat*
sen-jaku 選択	*to select*
sep-pou 説法	*giving discourse*
sha-ba 娑婆	Saha
shi-chi 四智	*four wisdoms*
shichi-so 七祖	*Seven Masters, the*
shi-nyo-mi-roku 次如弥勒	*subsequently being the same as Maitreya*
shi-shin 至心	*true heart*
shin-gyou 信楽	*joyous faith*
shin-jin 信心	*Faith*
shin-jin-ou-jou 信心往生	*birth of going through Faith, the, going to be born through Faith*
shou-dou-mon 聖道門	*gate of the path of sages*

shou-jou-ju-ni-juu-su-(ru) 正定取に住す（る）	*resides within the gathering of the rightly established*
shou-ka 証果	*effect that is Enlightenment, the*
shou-kaku 正覚	*true awakening*
shou-myou 称名	*praising (saying) the Name, repeating the Name, saying the Name, voiced utterance of the Name*
shou-toku-tai-shi 聖徳太子	Prince Regent Shotoku
shu-jou 衆生	*sentient beings*
shuk-ke 出家	*abandoning the world*
sou-gou 相好	*desirous attributes*
ta-riki 他力	*Other-power*
ta-riki-e-kou-no-sukui 他力回向の救い	*salvation by the transference of merit of Other-power*
ta-riki-hon-gan 他力本願	*Primal Vow of Other-power*
ta-riki-hon-gan-no-sukui 他力本願の救い	*salvation through the Other-power of the Primal Vow*

ta-riki-no-sukui 他力の救い	*salvation of Other-power*
tai-en 退縁	*conditions for regression*
tai-ten 退転	*retrogression*
ten-jin-bo-satsu 天親菩薩	Vasubandhu Bodhisattva
ton-yoku 貪欲	*passion of greed*
tou-kaku-i 等覚位	*level of being similar to awakening*
tou-shou-kaku 等正覚	*being similar to one truly awakened*
tou-shou-kaku-i 等正覚位	*level of being similar to one truly awakened*
tou-shou-kaku-no-kurai-ni-tsuku 等正覚のくらいにつく	*reaching the level of being similar to true awakening*
tou-yaku 当益	*benefit that will come, Benefit to come, future benefit*
wa-zen 汚染	*soiled and stained*
waku 惑	*confused*
yui-shin-doku-datsu-no-michi 唯信独達の道	*path of uniquely achieving with just faith, the*
zai-aku 罪悪	*criminal(ly) evil*

zai-aku-shou-ji 罪悪生死	*criminally evil filled with birth-and-death*
zai-aku-shou-ji-no-bon-bu 罪悪生死の凡夫	*foolish being of criminal evil and of birth-and-death, foolish being that is (filled with the) criminal evil of birth-and-death*
zen-dou-dai-shi 善導大師	Great Teacher Shan Tao, the
zen-toku-se-myou 全徳施名	*Name that bestows all virtues*
zui-ki-sep-pou 隋機説法	*explanation of the Dharma while considering the person being taught*

ABOUT THE AUTHOR

Professor Kyoshin Asano was born on October 12, 1929 in Hokkaido prefecture, Japan. He graduated from Ryukoku University in 1958 and continued his studies at the Hongwanji's Shuugaku-in, graduating in 1962. Following his studies he began a long teaching carrier at Ryukoku University. At Ryukoku University he also served as the head of the Department of Shinshu Studies while maintaining both undergraduate, graduate and Doctorate level courses. Because of his continued research and studies, even while teaching at Ryukoku University, he would achieve the title of *Kangaku*. As *Kangaku*, Kyoshin Asano is recognized as one of the foremost scholars of Shin Buddhism in the world. After his retirement from Ryukoku University he returned to serve at the temple founded by his father in Hokkaido, Japan.

His publications include:

shinran shonin hen saihou shinanshou no kenkyuu ("Research on Shinran Shonin's writing, Excerpts on the Directive to the Western Direction"), 1987
shinran to joudokyougi no kenkyuu ("Research on Shinran and the Pure Land Teachings"), 1988
kouhon saihou you ketsu ("Lectures on the Fundamental Establishment of the Western Direction"), 1993
kenjoudoshinjitsugyou monrui, shiryou hen, ("Passages on Practice that Reveal the Truth and Reality of the Pure Land, Volume on Research Materials"), 1999

He was also the chief editor of the key word search indexes for the following major Pure Land Buddhist Texts:
1982-*kangyoushijoushou* ("Explication of the Contemplation Sutra in Four Tablets")
1994-anrakushu ("Collection of Passages on Assurance and Joy")

Kyoshin Asano

1981-senjaku nenbutsu-shu ("Collection of Passages on the Selected Nenbutsu Path")

A NOTE ON THE TRANSLATION

Most Buddhist and Jodo Shinshu technical terms have been translated into English and appear as italicized text. Exceptions to this rule include proper nouns and those terms that have become part of the everyday vernacular. An alphabetical listing of these translated technical terms, whether italicized or not, are found in the appendix section together with the Japanese original and its romanized reading. Certain technical terms have been translated into different English terms for readability. Each of these different translations also appear listed in the appendix.

Certain terms were not translated and were transliterated instead. These include terms like Namo Amida Butsu and Nenbutsu. These terms were not translated because of their common usage in the daily English service observances at Jodo Shinshu temples. Most transliterated terms indicate the long "u" sound. However, certain terms, because of common usage, do not always show the long "u" sound as in "Shonin" (with the long "u" sound the term would have been transliterated as "Shounin"). Terms lacking the long "u" sound have been indicated in the translator's notes.

Translator's Notes

1   *Six paths* is being used as the literal translation for roku-dou (六道). Others have also translated the term as "six worlds" or "six realms (of existence)"

2   *Passion* is the translation for Bonnou (煩悩). Although it is often translated as a plural term or "passions," the singular form was chosen to contrast with "Enlightenment" or the state one reaches when all the passions are eliminated.

3   The title "kyogyoshinsho" (this spelling is used in favor of "kyougyoushinshou" because of common usage) is the popular name for Shinran Shonin's chief writing. The full title of the work is "ken joudo shinjitsu kyougyoushou monrui" (see also note 8). The popular title for this work comes from the explanation of the contents of the merit transference of the form of going or teaching, practice, faith and Enlightenment (kyou, gyou, shin, shou).

4   In Japan he is known as Ryuju (龍樹). This spelling is used in favor of "Ryuuju" because of common usage.

5   In Japan he is known as either Tenjin (天親) or Seshin (世親).

6   In Japan, the three priests from China are known as Donran (曇鸞), Doushaku (道綽) and Zendou (善導). Doushaku and Zendou are more commonly transliterated as "Doshaku" and "Zendo" respectively.

7   Honen Shonin's title or "Shonin (上人)" was not translated as in the others listed because of the standard usage of "Honen Shonin" (the spelling "Shonin" was chosen over "Shounin" because of common usage). However, if his title were translated as the others, then his name would have appeared as, "The Superior Person Honen." The title for Shinran, although it is pronounced the same way as the title for Honen Shonin, is written as 聖人. This title has the meaning of "sage." Thus, if Shinran Shonin's title were translated he would be referred to as, "The Sage Shinran."

8   The title in Japanese is "Ken Joudo Shinjitsu Kyou Gyou Shou
    Monrui (顕浄土真実教行証文類)." The translated title or
    "Passages on the Teaching, Practice and Enlightenment That
    Reveal the Truth and Reality of the Pure Land" can also be
    rendered as "Passages That Reveal the True and Real Teaching,
    Practice and Enlightenment of the Pure Land." This second
    reading is supported by the opening line of the Chapter on
    Teaching that states that with regards to "the *merit transference
    of the form of going* there is the True and Real Teaching, Practice
    and Enlightenment." The former reading, however, was selected
    because of its emphasis on the importance of the Pure Land in
    Shinran Shonin's thought, and how it more clearly emphasizes the
    focus on *Other-power* which the other rendering does not
    necessarily suggest. In reference to the structure of the text and
    the title chapters of the first four chapters of the text, the work is
    also known as the Kyougyoushinshou (although it is more
    commonly transliterated as "Kyogyoshinsho"). Among Shinran
    Shonin's many writings this work is central. With the meaning of
    being foundational to the teachings called Jodo Shinshu this text
    is also referred to as the "Primary Scripture." (see also note 3)

9   The Seven Masters are Nagarjuna Bodhisattva (Ryuju Bosatsu),
    Vasubandhu Bodhisattva (Tenjin Bosatsu), the Great Teacher Tan
    Luan (Donran Daishi), the Meditation Master Tao Cho (Doshaku
    Zenji), the Great Teacher Shan Tao (Zendo Daishi), the Regal
    Priest Genshin (Genshin Souzu), and the Superior Person Honen
    (Honen Shonin). (see also notes 4-7)

10 Here, "*transfers*" has the meaning of "using" or "applying" the
    merits earned or accumulated towards the goal of *going to be
    born*.

11 It is called the *cover of doubt* because it is that which keeps the
    heart of the Buddha, the source of faith, from entering in. It is not

a cover that keeps doubt *out*, but the cover that keeps the state of doubt *in*.

12 Zendo (this spelling is used in favor of Zendou because of common usage) is the traditional reading used by Jodo Shinshu. The Chinese pronunciation is Shan Tao (see also note 6).

13 Asogi is a Sanskrit term that has the meaning of "uncountable" and is used to emphasize the tremendous length of time that a kalpa is.

14 The four wisdoms refer to the four types of wisdom that a Buddha possesses. These four are: (1) the *great perfect mirror wisdom*, or the wisdom that is like a great mirror that perfectly reflects all things, (2) the *wisdom of equality*, or the wisdom that allows Buddha to treat all equally, it is also the wisdom that allows the Buddha to be free from making the distinction between self and others, (3) the *wisdom of wondrous contemplation*, or the wisdom that allows the Buddha to be able to contemplate all *dharma* (form) in its true state, and (4) the *wisdom of accomplishing metamorphosis*, or the wisdom that allows the Buddha to perform various manifestations to aid in the salvation of unenlightened beings.

15 The three bodies of a Buddha are (1) the *Dharma body*, or the body that is not limited by form and is identical with truth itself, (2) the *recompense body*, or the body that is manifested through fulfilling Vows, and (3) the *responsive body (transformative body)* or the body that is manifested to directly address unenlightened beings. This body is often equated with Sakyamuni Buddha.

16 The ten kinds of power or abilities associated with the Buddha's Wisdom are (1) the ability to distinguish right from wrong, (2) the ability to understand karma so deeply that its results can be known, (3) the ability to comprehend the various kinds of

meditations, (4) the ability to ascertain the strengths and weaknesses of people, (5) the ability to ascertain what people are understanding, (6) the ability to know the lineage of people, (7) the ability to understand the law of rebirth, (8) the ability to remember completely the past, (9) the ability to know about the births and deaths of people throughout the three periods of time (past, present, future), and (10) the ability to know how to eradicate afflictions from both self and others.

17 The four strengths refer to the four kinds of virtues that a Buddha (or Bodhisattva) has in being able to transmit the Dharma without fear. These four are (1) the ability for the Buddha to declare that the Buddha is someone who is ultimate in their wisdom without fear, (2) the ability of the Buddha to clearly state that all *passion* has been eradicated without fear, (3) the ability of the Buddha to be able to explain about the various kinds confused karma (that leads to confusion or suffering) without fear, and (4) the ability to talk about the three learnings of precepts, meditation, and wisdom that are designed to stop wrong behavior, to quiet the calculating mind, and to tear through the mind of confusion respectively without fear.

18 Desirous attributes refer to the physical attributes of a Buddha. These are described as the thirty-two attributes and as the eighty marks of the Buddha.

19 The Buddha's attribute of light is synonymous with Wisdom. It is the external physical manifestation of the internal virtue of wisdom.

20 Giving discourse is the "work" of a Buddha to transmit the truth that a Buddha has awakened to. It is one of the means utilized by a Buddha to save unenlightened beings.

21 Giving benefits, in this context, refers to the method by which Buddha (and Bodhisattva) are able to save unenlightened beings or, in other words, how Buddha (and Bodhisattva) give benefits to unenlightened beings so that they may be saved.

22 This six practice methodology taken together as a group is called the *"six paramita"* or the *six perfections*.

23 "the effect that is Enlightenment" is a translation for 証果 (shou-ka). The first character, shou, is the character that is used to refer to the state of Enlightenment. The second character, ka, has the meaning of effect or result. The unique characteristic of Jodo Shinshu's understanding of Enlightenment (the result) is how it is associated with its cause or faith.

24 The fifty-two steps of becoming a Buddha are divided into five "stages." These stages, from lowest to highest, are the stages of "faith (信)," "residence (住)," "practice (行)," "transference (回向)," and "being grounded (地)." Each of these stages is comprised of ten steps or levels. Of the fifty-two steps, then, the stage of faith is comprised of steps one through ten, the stage of residing from eleven to twenty, the stage of practice from twenty-one to thirty, the stage of transference from thirty-one to forty, and the level of being grounded from forty-one to fifty. Following these first fifty stages is the stage of being "similar to" or "equivalent to" Enlightenment. The final stage is "Wondrous Awakening" or Buddha-hood. The ten levels of Bodhisattva are the same as the ten levels found in the stage of being grounded or, in other words, the forty-first to the fiftieth stage.

25 Saha has the meaning of "endure." The Saha world is described as a world where the beings of that land all have to endure various pains and afflictions that are caused from both internal and external sources. The internal sources of suffering are due to the

various *passions* that all beings of that land are said to possess. The wind, rain, heat and cold that the beings of that land have to endure describe the external sources of suffering. This is the world where Sakyamuni Buddha taught the Dharma. In other words, it is the world we live in or a world where all beings are forced to endure both the internal and external sources of suffering.

Printed in Great Britain
by Amazon